# ANTHROPOLOGY
# IN PRACTICE

# Directions in Applied Anthropology:
## Adaptations and Innovations

Timothy J. Finan, Series Editor
Bureau of Applied Research in Anthropology,
University of Arizona, Tucson

# ANTHROPOLOGY IN PRACTICE

## Building a Career Outside the Academy

Riall W. Nolan

LYNNE
RIENNER
PUBLISHERS

BOULDER
LONDON

Published in the United States of America in 2003 by
Lynne Rienner Publishers, Inc.
1800 30th Street, Boulder, Colorado 80301
www.rienner.com

and in the United Kingdom by
Lynne Rienner Publishers, Inc.
3 Henrietta Street, Covent Garden, London WC2E 8LU

**Library of Congress Cataloging-in-Publication Data**
Nolan, Riall W.
    Anthropology in practice: building a career outside the academy / Riall Nolan.
      p.  cm.—(Directions in applied anthropology)
    Includes bibliographical references and index.
    ISBN 978-1-55587-957-0 (hc : alk. paper)
    ISBN 978-1-55587-985-3 (pb : alk. paper)
    1. Applied anthropology—Methodology.  2. Applied anthropology—Vocational
guidance.  I. Title.  II. Series.
GN397.5.N63   2003
301—dc21

                                                            2002073968

**British Cataloguing in Publication Data**
A Cataloguing in Publication record for this book
is available from the British Library.

Printed and bound in the United States of America

The paper used in this publication meets the requirements
of the American National Standard for Permanence of
Paper for Printed Library Materials Z39.48-1992.

5  4  3  2

# CONTENTS

# FIGURES AND TABLES

## Figures

## Tables

# PREFACE

This is a book for anthropology students who would like to become practitioners. Since the 1980s, thousands of anthropology's most talented graduates have become practitioners, breaking new and exciting ground on many fronts. Pioneers in the application of disciplinary knowledge to contemporary problems, they work outside the academy in hundreds of diverse settings on a host of important problems.

The need for well-qualified practitioners can only grow in the coming years. Today, we interact daily with people whose existence we hardly suspected only a few short years ago. Some of our new neighbors in the global village are friendly, others less so. We must approach our relationships with all of them responsibly. One thing is now very clear: success in the twenty-first century will not depend primarily on economic or military power, but on the ability to manage cultural differences productively.

We must manage these differences in order to resolve an array of issues—poverty, the environment, health care, collective security—for which there will probably never be simple, uniform, and orthodox solutions. Solutions will only come through understanding cultural diversity as a resource rather than an obstacle, a task for which anthropology is ideally suited.

Anthropology's message is both simple and compelling: there are other minds in the world and they think as well as ours; but they often think very differently. Anthropology allows us to explore—and ultimately, to understand—other cultural realities. Anthropology shows us the rationale and pattern behind different ways of living and thinking.

And anthropological practice, in particular, shows us how to put that knowledge to productive use.

The irony of our times, however, is that while opportunities for anthropologist practitioners have never been more abundant, few anthropology graduates are trained specifically for the demands of practice. Teaching materials oriented toward practice that talk specifically about what practitioners do and how they do it are scarce. Few anthropology instructors have significant experience of practice, and practitioners themselves are largely absent from university training programs.

The result is that most anthropology graduates—unlike, say, their counterparts in business, medicine, law, or engineering—enter the job market underprepared for the challenges and opportunities that await them. Instead, with a few notable exceptions, anthropological training in the United States prepares students primarily for careers as academics.

This situation, in essence, was the impetus for this book: to provide anthropology students and recent graduates with a glimpse at the alternative to an academic career, together with some practical suggestions for carrying anthropology beyond the walls of the university and putting it to work in the world. What I've written here isn't intended to challenge traditional anthropological training, but to complement and enhance it. The overall goal is quite simple: to ensure that if you want to become a practicing anthropologist, you are as well prepared as possible.

This book is intended for three groups of people. The first is undergraduates who have become interested in anthropology and want to make use of it, but are wondering, as many do, what they can actually do with an anthropology degree. The second group is graduate students. They are somewhat more confident of their ability to use anthropology, but may be uncertain about the career prospects for someone outside of university employment. The third group is that of recent graduates who are interested in making the transition from academically based research and teaching to the world of practice.

A single book can't tell you everything you need to know about practice; the field is too complex and dynamic. What I've tried to do instead is to provide some broad guidance and perspective, gleaned from my own experience and that of others, on what you can do to prepare yourself for a career in practice and to succeed. I've tried to anticipate the kinds of framing decisions you'll need to make, in graduate school and beyond, and to provide some simple guidelines for choice. Your own intelligence and energy will do the rest.

The book has six chapters and an appendix. Chapter 1, "Anthropological Practice," provides an overview of what practice is, looks at what distinguishes practitioners from academic anthropologists, and notes some current issues and controversies. Chapter 2, "Preparation for the Field," outlines how anthropology graduate students can prepare themselves for careers outside the university. Chapter 3, "Career Planning," discusses shaping your professional future, looking both at the strategic decisions to be made and at the information-gathering techniques that underlie these decisions. Chapter 4, "Getting In: Finding Your Job," takes you through the process of getting your first assignment as a practitioner. Chapter 5, "Work Survival: Organizations, Management, and Ethics," centers primarily on your first year at work, and discusses how to both survive and thrive. Chapter 6, "Making It Count: Advancing the Profession," looks broadly at how practitioners can advance their profession and their discipline, while at the same time contributing to wider society. The Appendix, "Resources for Further Learning," provides lists of helpful websites and publications relating to practice.

Through the work of practitioners, we are redefining the scope and content of anthropology for the twenty-first century. Practice draws on skills, knowledge, and approaches that range far beyond the traditional boundaries of anthropology, even as the processes and products of practice remain uniquely anthropological.

Globalization, like most social transformations, does not have pre-ordained outcomes. Instead, it presents us with opportunities as well as threats, together with a host of novel and compelling choices. To make those choices, the world does not really need more anthropologists—it needs anthropological practitioners, professionals capable of translating our discipline's considerable insights into useful ideas for building our collective future.

The first generation of anthropologist practitioners is already at work in the world. It is the next generation of practitioners who will secure anthropology's place in the great public forum. We owe it to them—and to our society—to begin preparing them for the important tasks that lie ahead.

This book is offered as a modest contribution toward that end.

# ACKNOWLEDGMENTS

B ridget Julian provided the impetus for this book and helped in many ways to shape both its form and its content. She is the kind of editor every writer wishes for but few ever find, and I feel honored to have been able to work with her. Thank you, Bridget; this is your book as much as mine.

The training of future anthropologists is perhaps the single most important task facing the discipline today. Concerns about training and career preparation have engaged the interest and creativity of a large number of anthropologist practitioners and academics sympathetic to practice. Many of these people are my friends and colleagues and have helped me formulate many of the ideas that went into this project.

In particular, I would like to thank the following for their suggestions, encouragement, and advice: Mitch Allen, Susan Allen, Adele Anderson, Ann Ballenger, Linda Bennett, Dean Birkenkamp, Peter Castro, Michael Cernea, Noel Chrisman, L. Davis Clements, Lisa Colburn, Cathleen Crain, Ted Downing, Shirley Fiske, Emilia Gonzalez-Clements, David Gow, Susan Hamilton, Michael Horowitz, Rebekah Hudgins, Stan Hyland, Ann Jordan, Dolores Koenig, Eliot Lee, Terry Leonard, Laurie Price, Bill Roberts, Patricia Sachs, Ted Scudder, Jeanne Simonelli, Neil Tashima, Tim Wallace, Rob Winthrop, and John Young. Each of you, in different ways, has worked hard to put anthropology to work for the needs of society, and to encourage students to do the same.

Finally, a special thanks to James Beebe and Sandy Ervin, who provided detailed, extensive, and very helpful comments on a late draft of this book.

—R. W. N.

# 1

# ANTHROPOLOGICAL PRACTICE

This chapter provides an overview of anthropological practice. The first section looks at how the practice option developed within anthropology, and what the field of practice looks like today. The second section looks at how practitioners work, and what distinguishes them from other sorts of specialists. The third section looks in some detail at how anthropological practitioners and their academic colleagues differ from one another. Section four takes up several of the current controversies and issues concerning practice that engage the attention of both academics and practitioners. The chapter concludes with a section on the attributes of successful practitioners, and some myths about practice.

## The Practice Option

### Antecedents

There has always been an applied side to anthropology. Early British social anthropology, as we know, was highly practice-oriented. In the United States, the New Deal, and later World War II itself, provided anthropologists with many opportunities to use what they knew in government service.

Anthropological practice, however, is a relatively recent phenomenon. Anthropological practitioners are individuals (generally with either an M.A. or a Ph.D.) who make their living applying anthropology in nonuniversity settings. In 1968 only 25 percent of new anthropology Ph.D.s in the United States took nonacademic positions. By 1995, however, it was estimated that more than 60 percent of M.A. and Ph.D. anthropologists were working outside the academy.[1]

Today, there are thousands of practitioners, working in a wide variety of sectors, doing an enormous number of different types of jobs. Every year, between one-quarter and one-half of all new anthropology M.A.s or Ph.D.s enter nonuniversity employment, and the market is strong. The *Chronicle of Higher Education* noted:

> Increasing globalization and racial and ethnic diversity are opening up new opportunities for cultural anthropologists in nongovernmental organizations, public-health organizations, and a variety of businesses, such as consulting, public-relations, and opinion-polling companies, to name but a few. Meanwhile an increasing number of Ph.D.s in the field are finding jobs in federal and state law-enforcement agencies, especially in forensic anthropology, and in private and government research laboratories as biological anthropologists.[2]

Within the academy, a small but growing literature focuses on practice and the training of practitioners. Outside the academy, organizations and networks that support practice have grown up, helped along by the Internet and the World Wide Web.

What is interesting is not that practice has grown, but that it took so long to appear. After all, it is not as if opportunities for extra-academic involvement were lacking in the United States or elsewhere during the latter half of the twentieth century. The Society for Applied Anthropology (SfAA) was founded in 1941, partly in response to these opportunities. Some of the best writing on the application of anthropology to problems of development and change dates from the period of the late 1940s to the early 1960s, when anthropologists were active both domestically and overseas as administrators, consultants, and trainers. Several significant projects in applied anthropology were done during this time, notably the Fox Project in the United States and the Vicos Project in Peru.

But anthropology graduates were slow to take advantage of this growth in opportunities. For one thing, U.S. universities were steadily expanding during the 1950s and 1960s. This provided academic jobs for anthropology graduates, inviting them to choose research and teaching over application, and to develop theory rather than practice.

Coupled with this academic expansion was the overall effect of the Vietnam War. Early involvements of anthropologists with defense- and intelligence-related programs triggered a firestorm of criticism from the academy and the professional associations. Anthropologists, by and large, opposed the war, and became increasingly reluctant to involve themselves in government-sponsored work. All of this produced a retreat from many aspects of applied work—especially if it involved the government.

Eventually, of course, university growth slowed. And although initially many anthropology graduates probably entered practice out of necessity, more and more of them began to choose nonacademic careers as the opportunities and rewards of practice became evident. In the mid-1980s, John van Willigen observed: "It appears unlikely that the large numbers of anthropologists entering the job market as practicing anthropologists now will take academic jobs in the future. They will not return because there will not be jobs for them, their salary expectations can not be met, and they just do not want to."[3]

His prediction proved accurate. Today, the concept of the anthropologist practitioner—a full-time professional working outside the university—is well established, and practice is no longer a secondary or alternative career for graduates. The demand for their services is strong, and continues to grow.

What accounts for the rapid growth of practice? Overproduction, for one thing. In the words of one observer, anthropology in the 1950s and 1960s was a "cat and rat farm," able and willing to absorb its graduates back into the academy, even though substantial opportunities existed even then for nonacademic employment. University hiring eventually slowed, but the production of graduates did not.[4]

Beginning in the 1960s, the growth of both international and domestic development programs fuelled an enormous increase in the demand for what might be called "social knowledge." Social-service agencies, schools, hospitals, and other organizations needed the kinds of information that anthropologists were well equipped to provide. As networks of practitioners began to form and practitioners began to appear regularly as presenters and discussants at the yearly meetings of the American Anthropological Association (AAA) and SfAA, more and more graduates found it both possible and attractive to consider nonacademic careers.

The growth of practice led to changes in the structure of the discipline. The journal *Practicing Anthropology* began publication in

1978. In the following year, the AAA passed the "Resolution in Support of Anthropologists Working Outside Academia," and began to include practitioners in their directory. The University of Kentucky began the Anthropology Documentation Project, collecting and cataloguing applied materials. In 1984, the National Association for the Practice of Anthropology (NAPA) was formed.

Local practitioner organizations, or LPOs, began to spring up in major cities, in part because of a feeling that the large, academically dominated national organizations were not responsive enough to issues of practice.[5] One of the first LPOs was the Society of Professional Anthropologists (SOPA), founded in 1973 in Tucson. The Washington Association of Practicing Anthropologists (WAPA) followed shortly thereafter. More recently, private-sector firms run by anthropologists have appeared, offering their services to the market.

A literature began to arise describing the activities of a very diverse group of practitioners working in a wide variety of contexts across the globe. Within this literature, several important themes emerged. One was the need for anthropologists to learn new things— and especially new ways of working—if they were to be professionally successful and effective outside the academy. Another was the need to refine and develop their guidelines for ethical practice. A third concerned the content and philosophy of training for anthropology students. A fourth was the link—or lack thereof—between practice as an activity in the field and anthropological theory building. And finally, concern began to surface concerning the relationship between the growing body of independent practitioners and the academy.

## Distinctions

Practice is now a full-time occupation for thousands of anthropologists. But how exactly are practitioners different from other anthropologists?

In the anthropological literature, a great deal of discussion has taken place about who is a "practicing" anthropologist, and how exactly such roles can be defined. It is helpful to think of anthropologists with interests in the use of anthropology as falling into three fairly distinct categories: academic anthropologists, applied anthropologists, and practitioners.

*Academic anthropologists* are university-based anthropologists who may, from time to time, participate in applied activities—typically as short-term consultants or expert witnesses. For this type of more traditional anthropologist, application is interesting and important, but essentially peripheral.

*Applied anthropologists* are also university-based anthropologists, but their interests center on applied areas, and their teaching, research, and extramural activities reflect these interests. Many do short-term consulting from home. A few have their own consulting business.

*Anthropologist practitioners* are people with advanced degrees in anthropology, but with no permanent or secure attachment to an academic institution. The application of anthropology is central to their work, but they may or may not have the title of "anthropologist." They work independently, or for government, private, or nonprofit organizations.

The essential distinction in this formulation is between anthropologists working from a university base and those who work outside the university. Within the university, applied anthropologists are in effect a subset of academic anthropologists (Figure 1.1).

This is not to say, of course, that anthropologists cannot move back and forth between practice and the academy over the course of their careers. But an anthropologist will have either a base in the university or a base in the world of practice, and where that base is located will determine important things about what one does and

**Figure 1.1   Different Types of Anthropology**

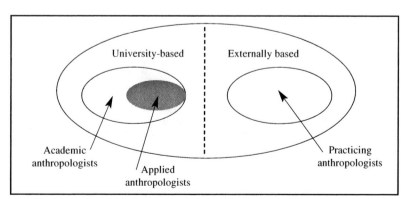

how one's work is judged. This can be seen more clearly in Table 1.1.

## The Shape of the Field

What do practitioners actually do? Here we have very inadequate data, but some broad indicators. NAPA's 1990 membership survey looked at where practitioners worked and what they did (Figure 1.2). The NAPA survey included large numbers of people who were not,

**Table 1.1    Differences Between Academic, Applied, and Practicing Anthropologists**

|  | Place of Employment | Core Activities | Who Judges Results |
|---|---|---|---|
| Academic anthropologists | Academically employed. | Research, grant writing, publication, and teaching. Topics forming the core of one's work are often, although not always, centered on the traditional academic pursuits of ethnography and theory. | Inside the academy, evaluations are done by peers, tenure committees, and review boards. Outside the academy, evaluations are done by peer reviewers (for publications or grants) and members of professional bodies. |
| Applied anthropologists | Academically employed in most cases; operate as a temporary consultant outside the university, at times and in situations of their own choosing. The university is used as a base of operations and a refuge. | Similar to the above, but with the addition of activities performed on behalf of outside constituencies. These include training, consulting, advocacy, research, etc. | Results are ultimately judged by one's peers inside the academy. The assessments of outside constituents, although important in many cases, do not usually adversely affect one's career or job security. |
| Practicing anthropologists | Self-employed in many cases; employees of agencies and corporations in others. | Activities are widely varied, and change according to the assignment. They include research, management, evaluation, training, consulting, advocacy, etc. | Employers and clients judge results, usually according to their own standards. The results of evaluation have direct consequences for future jobs or assignments. |

**Figure 1.2    What Practitioners Do and Where They Work**

### What Practitioners Do

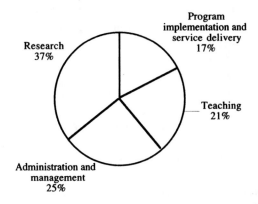

### Where Practitioners Work

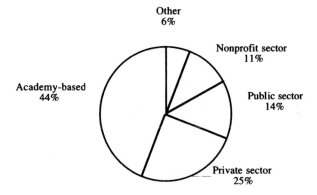

*Source:* Adapted from Baba 1994; Fiske 1991.

strictly speaking, practitioners. This accounts for the high proportion of university-based respondents. Nevertheless, it is interesting to note the number of practitioners in the private sector, which includes, by the way, people working as independent consultants.

These data, while crude, do indicate something of the shape of the field. Today's practitioners include people working in a wide range of organizations, and in a variety of sectors, both here and overseas. Once mainly valued for their data-collection skills or their knowledge of specific communities or populations, practitioners are now involved in policy formulation, in the implementation of plans and programs, and in review, monitoring, and assessment activities. To an increasing extent, they are decisionmakers within the organizations for which they work. Few of the jobs they do have the word "anthropologist" in the title.

Practitioners' professional roles can therefore be defined with respect to three principal axes: a *base* from which one operates; a *sector* within which one is primarily active; and one or more *functions* that one performs within that sector (Figure 1.3).[6]

The examples listed above do not exhaust the possibilities, and are meant to be illustrative rather than definitive. In reality, many practice jobs are composed of multiple elements that shift in importance over time as programs and projects develop. I once worked, for example, for a Washington-based consulting firm where I had the title of "socioeconomic planner." My firm sent me to the U.S. Agency for International Development (USAID) in Tunis, where I was listed as

**Figure 1.3   Principal Components of Anthropological Practice**

| BASE | SECTOR | FUNCTION |
|---|---|---|
| Government | Social services | Management |
| Corporate | Public administration | Production/implementation |
| Nonprofit | Agriculture | Design |
| Independent/free-lance | Environment/natural | Evaluation/impact |
| Sole proprietorship | resources | assessment |
| Small business | International development | Data collection/analysis |
| University | Manufacturing | Needs assessment |
| | Advertising | Advocacy |
| | Pubic relations | Policy formulation |
| | Marketing | |
| | Planning | |

*Source:* Adapted from American Anthropological Association 1982; and Omohundro 1998, p. 32.

"contractor—technical assistance." USAID in turn assigned me to work with the Tunis city government, where I had the title "*directeur du projet.*" In this capacity I designed and managed an urban development program that addressed health, small business development, literacy, and women's vocational training. In addition to design and management, my work included data collection and analysis, negotiation with government and community leaders, and training. Such multidimensionality is typical of many practitioner jobs.

## The Practitioner's Art

### Practice as Negotiated Problem Solving

Donald Schön has described the topography of practice as a wet and messy swamp, with a dry knoll rising out of it. On the dry ground, high above everything else, problems are solved in a relatively clean and smooth fashion, using research-based theory and technique. The problems on the high knoll tend to be technically interesting but relatively unimportant to humanity at large.[7]

Down in the swamp, however, the problems are disordered, messy, and confusing, and usually resist purely technical solutions. But this is where the most important human issues lie, the ones that can't be solved by technique and theory alone, but through a combination of professional artistry and direct engagement with the issues. The scope and significance of the issues in the swamp are hardly ever clear at the outset, and few ready-made solutions are available. The stakeholders in such situations have differing and often competing interests, values, and perspectives.

In such situations, both the problems and solutions to the problems must be constructed—that is, built up through interaction and negotiation between the practitioner and the situation. Even where ends can be stated succinctly—e.g., "health," "well-being," "security," or "profit"—the terms themselves may conceal important differences in meaning and interpretation. Each situation, in a sense, becomes a special one, and a fresh test of the practitioner's ability to frame and deal with the particularities of the case at hand.

This is what Schön terms *reflective practice*—the process of negotiation between the practitioner and the surrounding context, leading to eventual resolution. Schön says:

> Skillful practitioners learn to conduct frame experiments in which
> they impose a kind of coherence on messy situations and thereby
> discover consequences and implications of their chosen frames. . . .
> It is this ensemble of problem framing, on-the-spot experiment,
> detection of consequences and implications, back talk and response
> to back talk, that constitutes a reflective conversation with the
> materials of a situation—the designlike artistry of professional
> practice.[8]

## Anthropological Frames

Practitioners operate by framing problems, and then dealing with
what they find within the frame. And different sorts of practitioners
will frame problems quite differently. A problem in international
development might be seen by a nutritionist in one way, by an economist in another, and by a demographer in still another. Sometimes
these frames conflict. "When a pickpocket looks at a king," the
proverb says, "all he sees are his pockets."

So although we are in a sense constrained by the frames we construct, it is also the frames that let us see. What kinds of frames do
anthropologists bring to situations of practice?

*An approach grounded in context.*   Anthropologists build understanding from the ground up, rather than applying theory from
above. Anthropology students learn their craft firsthand through
intensive and interactive periods of fieldwork, and they carry this
approach with them into the world of practice.

This approach is inductive; meaning is not imposed *on* the situation, but emerges slowly over time *from* the situation. Anthropology
generates meaning through a process of discovery of what is there,
rather than verifying or confirming what we might assume is there.[9]

Although anthropology's approach is both qualitative and quantitative, it is the qualitative aspect that is particularly important. For
an anthropologist, raw data are relatively meaningless; their significance assumes shape and weight only within a particular cultural
context. Without an accurate understanding of context, the question
of what to count cannot be answered. As someone once pointed out,
if you're in a strange city and see someone winking at you across the
bar, you can always count the winks, but do you know what the
winks mean?

*Understanding rather than judgment.*  Anthropologists approach the task of gaining understanding in a nonjudgmental way, believing that tolerance and relativism are important methodological tools. Anthropologists not only document the differences in outlook that characterize human communities, but they explore the logic and coherence behind these differences. This can sometimes turn practitioners into iconoclasts, reminding their colleagues that all arrangements are essentially arbitrary, all assumptions open to question.

*Seeking connections both inside and out.*  Anthropologists look at a situation holistically. They seek connections and patterns, rather than attempting to isolate and segment phenomena. Anthropologists uncover these connections and patterns within the context of their work, but they also attempt to place what they learn into a wider context as well, comparing and contrasting what they have found in one situation with others. In this way they are often able to build up both a broad and deep understanding.

*The anthropological advantage.*  Today, humanity's most important undertakings depend in large measure not only on our ability to understand varieties of human experience and different ways of seeing the world, but on our skill at using this understanding effectively. The fact that human cultures are different, that aspects of a culture are connected, and that the differences and connections are important is at one level merely common sense. But anthropology's unique approach promotes *discovery*, *synergy*, and *sustainable solutions.*

• *Discovery:* When cultures connect—in the workplace, at school, or across the bargaining table—differences can quickly become evident. People from different cultures often do not see, interpret, or value things in the same way. They may have different goals, different methods for achieving those goals, and different standards with which to judge success or failure. Although such differences may be obvious on the surface, their deeper significance is rarely understood. Without the understanding that anthropological discovery can bring, workable solutions often remain out of reach.

• *Synergy:* Understanding difference, by itself, solves few problems. But anthropology in combination with other disciplines can be a powerful force for change. An engineer, for example, may know how to build roads, and an architect may know how to design houses. But this technical knowledge almost always requires local cultural understanding in order to work effectively. The engineer or architect may have little understanding of how villagers' use patterns affect the roads or buildings they construct; the doctor may not comprehend how local concepts of disease influence demands for health care; the economist may ignore symbolic or qualitative aspects of resource use and decisionmaking. Anthropologists help to make these connections, producing results that go beyond whatever a single approach might bring. In situations of practice, this synergy reappears repeatedly.

• *Sustainability:* In the same way, an approach to change that has been constructed on a solid base of contextual understanding is more likely to both respond to the needs of the moment and to continue to meet those same needs over time. As we know from long experience, it is relatively easy to innovate, but much harder to institutionalize.

Anthropology thus provides insight that complements rather than challenges other ways of knowing. This makes anthropological practitioners especially valuable in situations where different viewpoints exist, and where progress depends on the understanding and reconciliation of these viewpoints.

## Expertise and Practice

*The limitations of expertise.*   Because situations of practice are often messy and ambiguous, there is a temptation to rely on people who already claim to know the answers. Expert advice, after all, is authoritative advice. By relying on the models and procedures offered by experts, managers hope to avoid the risks and costs associated with an extended dialogue with the environment. And if one expert's advice does not suit, another, different opinion can usually be found.

But knowing "that" is not a substitute for knowing "how." In my own field of international development planning, for example, reliance on received models sometimes gives rise to an illusory sense on the part of project managers of certainty and control. But this is almost always disrupted, sooner or later, by the appearance of local factors, neither the existence nor the significance of which was accounted for by the model. This, indeed, is an important component of the literature on development.

Unlike many other specialists, anthropologist practitioners have little difficulty in acknowledging the primacy of such local factors, and in particular, the skill, creativity, and knowledge of the stakeholders affected by plans and projects.

Specialists must collaborate with these stakeholder groups—each possessing different resources and different degrees of power and influence—to achieve mutually acceptable outcomes. Collaboration becomes particularly important when one group plans for the supposed benefit of another. And collaboration requires the recognition that there will be different sorts of "experts" in any given situation (many of them without university degrees), and that to work together successfully, everyone will have to learn something more. For an anthropologist practitioner, engagement with the practice situation on its own terms is essential.

As anthropologist practitioners know, many situations of practice—whatever their apparently clean lines—are in reality an unfolding drama, played out against a background of diverse and shifting concerns. Whereas many specialist-experts attempt to *direct* the situation, anthropologist practitioners, as learners, tend rather to want to *interact* with it, and through interaction, to learn what it is important to know.

And whereas technical problems often simply require us to apply a formula, skill, or procedure that we already know, the emergent problems with which many anthropologists engage require new learning and new thinking, both of which take place on the spot.

As reflective practitioners, anthropologists assume that they do not know everything about the environment they are working in. They also assume that they do not fully understand, at the outset, how interventions in that environment will play out. They therefore tend to make learning a high priority, and to keep plans and arrangements as flexible as possible at the early stages of engagement. When mistakes occur, these, too, are treated as opportunities to learn.[10]

*Experts and learners.*   In these and other ways, anthropologist practitioners differ from other types of experts.

| **Technical Expert** | **Anthropologist Practitioner** |
|---|---|
| Usually deals with things. Outcomes are expressed as facts and expert opinions. | Usually deals with people. Outcomes center on cultural meanings and interpretations. |
| The expert "owns" his domain. He or she is expert because of his/her mastery of subject matter. The expertise is located in the person of the expert. | Expertise is located in the project context itself. The anthropologist possesses certain skills, but is primarily a conduit or an interpreter for meanings arising from this context. |
| Knowledge is bounded by disciplines and subject areas. Facts are "objective" and neutral. | Knowledge is a social construct, and not always conventionally bounded. The process of generating knowledge and meaning is a dialogue. |
| The expert is presumed to know, and must claim to know, regardless of any uncertainties. | The anthropologist is also presumed to know, but is not the only person to have relevant knowledge. Uncertainties can be a source of learning for all stakeholders. |
| The expert keeps a certain distance from the client, and maintains the expert's role. | The anthropologist must enter into the client's thoughts and feelings. |
| The expert looks for respect and status from the client. | The anthropologist looks for openness and a real connection with the client.[11] |

*How practitioners learn.* Practitioners learn experientially, in ways very similar to those that characterize anthropological fieldwork. This extended conversation—sometimes tense, always rich— between a practitioner and the environment is also characteristic of many other fields of professional endeavor, including musical performance, psychiatry, medicine, planning, and architecture (Figure 1.4).

Many of the factors that emerge as crucial for the resolution of problems are initially hidden. As practitioners negotiate with the

**Figure 1.4  Experiential Learning**

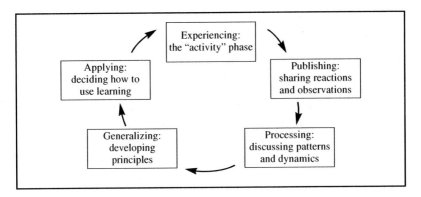

environment, these will emerge. The software of needs, perceptions, preferences, and expectations thus becomes matched to the hardware of the technical solutions available for responding to them.

Reflective practice is a process of gradual, interactive problem solving. Problems exist, not in abstract theory, but in a setting, a specific context. To solve the problem, practitioners must understand—and interact with—this context. Schön puts it this way: "The enquirer's relation to this situation is transactional. He shapes the situation, but in conversation with it, so that his own models and appreciations are also shaped by the situation. The phenomena that he seeks to understand are partly of his own making; he is in the situation that he seeks to understand."[12]

The task, in other words, is not simply to figure out how to solve a particular problem, but how to discover in the first place what the problem is, and how it should be approached. Far from being able to determine events and outcomes, practitioners are often unsure, at the outset, of what needs to be done, how this can be accomplished, and how the environment will react. Decisions are made incrementally, even as new information is appearing, in a manner more like intelligence gathering than research.

Often, of course, we fail to engage with the practice situation on its own terms. Under the multiple pressures of time, money, and bureaucratic expediency, specialists often import ready-made solutions—or pieces of them—into the environment, hoping that what has worked elsewhere will work again. Such an approach is attractive bureaucratically: it helps specialists deal with internal organizational requirements and procedures, and greatly reduces the time needed to deal—however superficially—with the problem at hand.

At the same time, however, such an approach is severely constraining: basic framing decisions tend to be made very early in the process of problem solving—often before the problem has been clearly understood—with little or no consideration of other possible options or approaches. In addition to limiting the range of outcomes obtained, such an approach may significantly raise the risk of failure.

Very few situations of practice are alike. What is correct in one environment may not be so in another. Furthermore, most situations of practice are not stable, but evolving, the product of a continual process of social negotiation. These negotiations usually involve exchange, barter, and co-optation, as well as less savory forms of interaction including manipulation, coercion, and deceit. Practice situations are often continually developing dramas, characterized by stress, emotion, and change.[13]

## Practice and the Academy

### Differences Between Academics and Practitioners

Academic anthropology is a discipline; anthropological practice a profession. Although connected, they operate in distinctly separate spheres. Let's look, therefore, at a few of the more important differences between the culture of the academy and that of the world of practice.

*Structures.*   Academics and practitioners work within different structures. For tenured faculty at least, the university is a highly patterned and secure environment, within which academics have considerable freedom and autonomy. Although lip service is paid to the virtues of collegiality, most academics tend to work mainly in isolation from one another.

Academic structures are relatively simple, and do not vary much from one institution to another. There are few ranks among the professorate, and it takes most of a professional lifetime to rise through them. The rules and values associated with these structures, although more complex, vary little from one place to another.

Job security for a college professor tends to center on the achievement of tenure, which at most institutions is conferred largely on the basis of published research judged acceptable by one's peers according to scholarly canons. Once tenure has been achieved, job security is very high, and is largely independent of fluctuations of the market or even the opinions of peers and colleagues. The privileges of academic rank are clearly defined, and tenured professors have near-total authority over relatively restricted domains.

In contrast, practitioners inhabit a much more diverse and changeable environment. Their workplaces are characterized by complex hierarchies, marked differences in rules and procedures from one organization to another, and multiple and shifting sets of stakeholder-clients with differing and sometimes conflicting interests.

Job security for practitioners depends not on publication, tenure, or teaching evaluations, but on achieving results on a continuing basis. Practitioners are paid by their employers or clients for what they can do, not necessarily for what they know. In a sense, a practitioner's reputation is only as good as his last assignment. The results practitioners produce are judged, not in academic terms, but according to the terms and needs of the market. As the market changes, so too will the criteria for success.

*Rewards and constraints.* University-based anthropologists are both rewarded and constrained by a well-defined system that is fairly uniform across the academy. An individual's status will depend on a collection of things, all of which are derived and assessed from within the academy itself. Promotion, tenure, and publication have already been mentioned. A position at one of the "elite" schools is another significant mark of status. An academic's personal reputation may be based on only one or two significant achievements, often occurring relatively early in one's career.

For practitioners, of course, it is different. In government and the private sector, where most practitioners are, what counts is the size and importance of the agency, firm, or corporation you work for, and your rank within it. And what counts most of all, in most organizations, is how close you are to the centers of power.

Within the academy, there is little direct pressure for results; timetables are geared to the academic year, funding cycles, and the seasons, and what is not finished in the spring term can usually wait until fall. Academics might be said to be essentially self-employed within a university support structure.

Practitioners, on the other hand, have a more finely honed sense of urgency. They work to deadlines set by clients, in situations where time is money. And while academics are judged, by and large, according to standards set by peers, practitioners are judged by standards set by clients and employers, who also provide them with rewards and recognition.

Whereas academics operate largely independently and with little direct or immediate accountability, practitioners usually work as part of a team, group, or organization; are often accountable to multiple sets of supervisors and colleagues; and must deal directly with the consequences of their actions and decisions.

*Activities and work styles.*    Academics and practitioners work in very different ways. Academics have problems and foci defined largely from within the discipline, while practitioners have problems defined from outside. Practitioners must produce acceptable results, quickly and efficiently, in collaboration with other specialists.

For academics, criticism is a very important part of academic discourse (which is, after all, essentially adversarial). Finding flaws is just as important for practitioners, not so much to sharpen the focus of the argument, but primarily in order to achieve effective results. The discourse of practice must, above all, be useful, not just theoretically interesting. Cris Johnsrud comments: "The ability to provide critical thinking is essential in industry and government, so that problems are understood. However, without the concomitant skill of suggesting ways to 'fix it' (which implies taking risks and making decisions) critique alone is inadequate."[14]

Policymakers deal with complex and often ambiguous situations. They therefore seek to simplify and prioritize elements of their environment—to limit, so to speak, the size of the playing field. Knowledge is primarily useful, not for its own sake, but to the extent that it helps people make decisions, justify decisions, or manipulate the context in which decisions are made. Getting results and moving things forward may therefore mean simplifying the messy nature of the situation. It may also mean not dealing with certain issues, or not questioning certain aspects of policy or procedure.[15]

Practitioners needing to made decisions of the moment will therefore tend to simplify reality, while academics may be intent on developing a more detailed understanding of that reality. Given a real-world planning problem, academics are inclined, by both training and temperament, to call into question basic aspects of the situation—aspects that practitioners themselves must usually accept as givens.

Whereas practitioners know that no plan is ideal, academics may present their arguments and scenarios in ideal and sometimes unrealistic terms. Academics who see their role as essentially providing information in a client-free, value-neutral context strike many practitioners as naïve.

These differences can be seen, for example, in the work produced by academics and practitioners. Academic anthropologists produce ethnographies, while practitioners mainly produce reports, summaries, and analyses. Some of the differences between them are summarized below.

| **Practitioner Reports** | **Academic Ethnographies** |
|---|---|
| Reports tend to be limited in scope and confined to the problem in hand. Reports are usually intended to be used for problem solving and decisionmaking. The time available for preparation is usually quite short, constrained by outside deadlines. | Ethnographies are often general, holistic, and wide-ranging. Their purpose may be primarily to add to theory and knowledge in general terms. There are no particular deadlines, unless they are academic or publishing ones. |
| Reports tend to be limited to that information necessary for action. Although qualitative material is not excluded, quantitative data are usually required as well, and often preferred. | Favors "thick description" and completeness in documentation. Some quantitative information is sought, but there is a great deal of qualitative data, and a great deal of interpretation. |
| Documents are often clearly partisan, and may openly advocate for one position or another. The analysis and discussion will often be directed toward a specific interpretation or conclusion. | Writing is self-consciously "value-neutral" to the greatest extent possible. The ethnographic data are presumed to speak for themselves. |

| Practitioner Reports | Academic Ethnographies |
|---|---|
| Future options should be laid out clearly and succinctly, together with their likely future consequences. Solutions proposed in reports are often not ideal ones, but the best possible options under the existing circumstances. | Typically, the future is not discussed very much in an ethnography. If it is, it is often highly speculative, and does not necessarily derive from the data presented. Since few ethnographies are problem-driven, few options are presented. If they are, they may be presented in "ideal" terms. |

*Self-definition.*   Academic anthropologists fit into a relatively well-defined role; they are specialists within a discipline that claims uniqueness as an all-embracing science of humanity.

Practitioners, in contrast, face important decisions about how to represent themselves and their work. On the one hand, defining one's contribution as somehow "unique" may promise more than it can deliver, and isolate the anthropologist from other specialists. On the other hand, making broad, sweeping, and unspecific claims may damage one's credibility.[16]

A good example of the latter occurred early in the heyday of development anthropology. A 1973 article carried this quote from a senior anthropologist (academically based, but with a considerable "applied" reputation) about what anthropology could do for development administrators:

> [The anthropologist's] most important contribution to action programs is an unusually broad and flexible field research methodology, based on a holistic view of society and culture and using general concepts such as cultural integration, cultural dynamics, socio-cultural systems in contact, and the premises underlying cultural forms as a means to structure research and interpret results. Anthropological field research is exploratory and wide ranging, and in contrast to the more elaborate research methods of other social sciences, it is relatively unstructured. But in directed culture change programs, where the technical, social, cultural, economic, psychological, and other pertinent factors are almost infinite and not usually recognized in advance, this exploratory quality is enormously advantageous. It vastly increases the investigator's chances

of hitting upon critical elements in any specific situation, simply because the anthropologist is trained to examine the entire spectrum of the culture he studies.

While there is nothing inherently wrong with this description of what anthropology does, the author's own comment was telling: "I found that [this formulation] left project administrators unimpressed. They wanted specific answers to hard questions of implementation. It is true, of course, that [he] is talking about information-gathering, but if the information cannot be translated into action, then the anthropologist will find himself ignored."[17]

Practitioners may be highly specialized, but they are usually only one specialist among many. Situations of practice require teamwork, the sharing of information, and accommodation to the views of others. Whereas practitioners are expected to "get on board" once decisions are made, academic anthropologists are sometimes viewed as incurable dissidents, continuing to raise questions that cannot be satisfactorily answered within the developing context of the project at hand.

Above all, a practitioner's work must be responsive to client needs. Michael Painter provides a most interesting example of how a practicing anthropologist (and the organization he worked for) viewed the proposed contribution of an academic anthropologist. I have quoted at length from Painter's account because I think it illustrates several aspects of academic/practitioner differences quite well.

While working for CABI, a South American NGO, Painter became

> more critical of the assertions that anthropologists conventionally make about the benefits of our research among grassroots organizations. For example, CABI recently received a research proposal from a well-respected social scientist . . .
>
> When the committee reviewed the proposal, it found that what the researcher wanted was for CABI to grant virtually unlimited access to its staff and its files, to help identify and contact people who would criticize the organization, and to provide transportation and logistical support. In return, the researcher would publish critical discussions about whether he thinks that CABI really does what it says it does or whether he thinks it is misleading itself and its constituency. While he would acknowledge CABI assistance, all publications would be in his name, and, because of his commitment to academic freedom, CABI would exercise no control over

the content or the quality of his publications. The researcher also offered to organize critical public discussions about CABI at his university. . . .

CABI informed the researcher that it was not in a position to host such a project at this time, and it suggested ways in which the researcher might refocus the project so that it would be able to offer an institutional affiliation. *The initial reaction of the researcher was indignation at what he saw as the effrontery of CABI to criticize his proposal and its lack of respect for his academic freedom.* To his credit, he did come to see that its concerns were not spurious, although he has not yet indicated whether he would be interested in reworking the project based on CABI's suggestions.[18] (emphasis mine)

## The Discipline's Poor Relation?

Despite its growth, anthropological practice remains the poor relation within the discipline, its connections with the academic mainstream unequal and uneasy. Debate continues within the academy, even today, about the definition of applied anthropology, its significance, and its relation to theory. With a few notable exceptions, applied anthropologists and practitioners have remained outside the discipline's inner circle, their work for the most part unpublished in the major journals and book series.

Some academic anthropologists still consider practice a lesser, somewhat debased form of anthropology, devoid of theory, lacking in methodological rigor, and fraught with ethical pitfalls. Within many if not most of today's university departments of anthropology, too much concern for and involvement with practical matters can adversely affect one's professional standing. The criteria for recruitment, promotion, and tenure inside university departments still tend, by and large, to favor research and theory over application.

Postmodernism in anthropology has sharpened the debate about the ethics of praxis. If, as some postmodernists claim, culture is a contested process rather than an empirical set of categories, then intervention is partisan, and incompatible with scholarship.[19] The more conservative within the discipline still heap scorn on popularizers, and warn students (and untenured faculty) of the dangers of losing one's anthropological soul to the attractions of worldly work.

In sum, for some academically based anthropologists, practice is something that graduates do if they cannot obtain academic positions. Marsha Jenakovich and Owen Murdoch note:

Both masters and Ph.D. students are primarily trained in anthropological methods of qualitative research, and it is assumed that those who will seek employment outside of academia will participate in some form of applied research. This kind of work has been most highly valued by the discipline. It is assumed that this is the kind of work to which all anthropologists aspire, and therefore those working in more practice-based settings must be doing so due to an inability to secure "real" (i.e., research-based) anthropological positions.[20]

Many practitioners, on the other hand, believe that the academy understands little of what they do or how they do it. The discipline, in their view, does not appreciate or understand the ethical issues they face, and ignores, for the most part, the methodological and theoretical contributions they make.

## Controversies and Issues

As one might imagine, the growth of practice has provoked discussion inside and outside the academy. Three issues predominate in this discussion: how practitioners are trained; what standards should apply to practice; and what the relationship should be between practice and the academy.

### Practitioner Training

In recent years, attention has started to focus on the discrepancies between the demands of practice and the type of anthropological training received by students in most graduate and undergraduate programs.

Most anthropology programs, including those that term themselves "applied," still train students primarily for the academic world. Most instructors in those programs are anthropologists with little if any experience of practice. One recent study looked at a sample of the largest anthropology programs in the country, and found that less than a third of them offered any courses in applied anthropology, and of those that did, only one university required the course.[21]

Fortunately, there are signs that this is beginning to change. There have been several recent calls from within the academy to reform the way anthropology is taught.[22] At the same time, students have become more vocal about their dissatisfactions with existing programs. Practitioners holding master's degrees have organized sessions at anthropology's national meetings to discuss training concerns, and several recent issues of *Practicing Anthropology* have focused specifically on issues of training for practitioners.

Some of the anthropology associations have responded to this concern. The National Association for the Practice of Anthropology, the National Association of Student Anthropologists, and the High Plains Association have all organized conference sessions and workshops on aspects of practice. In 1999, the Consortium on Applied Anthropology was formed between a dozen of the more progressive and innovative applied-anthropology programs, with a view toward improving the quality of training.

## Standards for Practice

Despite this growing response, there is little agreement among anthropologists as to what might constitute an essential core curriculum in applied or practicing anthropology, and even less agreement on what acceptable standards for this curriculum might be. Nor is there agreement on how—or even whether—practicing anthropologists might be certified. Indeed, attempts to devise some form of certification in recent years have provoked intense discussion and some controversy among both academic and nonacademic anthropologists.

Since standards for practice have never been clearly defined, it is difficult to see how training programs might be measured or evaluated against some common set of criteria. Who would prescribe these criteria, and on what basis? How would we know whether programs or curricula were adequate or not? How would we measure the performance of graduates from these programs? Do credentials—of whatever kind—depend more on how one is trained or on how well one uses the training? These and other related questions continue to be debated.

There are multiple and conflicting forces at work here that go far beyond the academy itself. Although the market for nonacademic anthropologists is expanding, that for academic anthropologists has remained essentially stagnant for years. Within academic disciplines in general, the bar for tenure has been raised steadily higher over the years. So at a time when opportunities for practicing anthropologists are growing, opportunities for the academically based anthropologists who control training are shrinking.

In a 1988 article, Max Drake expressed pessimism about the academy's ability or willingness to embrace practitioners. Instead, he noted a tendency among academics to restrict access to the "real" anthropology of the academy, by insisting, for example, that only refereed publications and orthodox research be recognized as legitimate for advancement. In this way, practice remains essentially illegitimate, its products are not true publications, and only the Ph.D. confers true status as an anthropologist.[23]

Several years later, Merrill Singer went even further when he suggested that postmodernism is an attempt by the academy to reassert control over a deteriorating situation:

> The whole discourse of postmodernism in anthropology privileges the doing and writing of ethnography as the very essence of anthropology's "work," while application evaporates as a component of the anthropological project. Indeed, the argument could be made that reasserting the primacy of university-based, theoretical anthropology is the hidden agenda of postmodernism within the discipline.[24]

Connected to this is the issue of standards of professional behavior. Although several statements of ethics exist for practitioners, these do not address some of the most important issues that practitioners face. There is no existing definition, in reality, of anthropological malpractice. More to the point, existing mechanisms provide little remedy for addressing even the most egregious breaches of behavior, should these occur.

## Relations Between Practice and the Academy

In these and other ways, there is a worrying degree of distance between the academy and the world of practice, quite different from many other disciplines. Drake notes:

> In professions like social work, psychology, and medicine individuals in research, clinical, and administrative specialties maintain strong ties and often exchange work experience. With anthropologists, practitioners are rarely offered posts at universities to teach practice. Their publications . . . do not count in academic circles.

> Academicians rarely seek the consultation of practitioners and often appear uninterested or contemptuous of practitioner skills.
>
> Practitioners are no better. We often hold our academic colleagues in contempt for their low salaries, their lack of willingness to take risks or exercise power, and their seeming unawareness of the world out there. We are often critical of their lack of relevance to the world of policy and contemptuous of their ignorance of administrative culture.[25]

There is an apparent attitude among many academics that the working world is somehow not as intellectually exciting as the academy, and that it is somehow ethically compromised by definition. Noting the appearance of "public-interest anthropology" as a topic for discussion at recent national meetings, Singer pointedly asks why mainstream academics seem so unaware of the variety of public-interest work that has been done for years by practitioners: "The answer lies in a conscious nonrecognition of applied anthropology. Judging from some introductory textbooks and journal articles, one could conclude that applied anthropology was only practiced during and shortly after WWII. While the work of anthropologists from that era is recognized and applauded, the next half-century of diverse efforts is all but disavowed."[26]

There exists virtually no effective channel for dialogue between practitioners and their academically based colleagues. The *American Anthropologist* rarely publishes articles by practitioners, or about practice, and the majority of the articles published in *Human Organization* are written by anthropologists working in universities. Neither journal regularly reviews books by practitioners. The *High Plains Journal* and *Practicing Anthropology* are, for the most part, the only regular publications in which practitioners find a strong voice.

At the yearly meetings of the AAA, practitioners appear rarely on the program, and few sessions focus on issues of practice. The Society for Applied Anthropology's annual meetings feature more participation by practitioners, but here again, the bulk of the membership is composed of university faculty, and meeting sessions reflect this.

The Applied Anthropology Documentation Project at the University of Kentucky is the only regularly published list of applied and practice-related materials, and this contains but a small fraction of the enormous amount of "gray literature" produced by practitioners.

Academics and practitioners clearly coexist in an uneasy relationship. Because few anthropology professors have deep experience with the world of practice, it is sometimes difficult for them to understand what their graduates do, and how their professional lives are constructed. Practitioners, for their part, often feel cut off from their academic roots, undervalued, and ignored. The grand debates that flourish within the academy do not seem to touch issues that are significant to them. The literature of the discipline does not, for the most part, speak to their concerns, or tell their stories. Jenakovich and Murdoch comment: "The discipline of anthropology and its body of practitioners seem to be ships passing in the night. They do not know each other; they are not connected. The two are seen as completely different (because they are)—one involves the production of knowledge, while the other involves the use of that knowledge."[27]

Although the differences between academic and practicing anthropology are significant and sometimes troubling, they can be a source of creativity and renewal, if managed intelligently. One of the main tasks for the future is therefore to craft and maintain a healthy reciprocal relationship between the two, based on mutual respect and understanding.

## Practice and You

### The Attributes of a Successful Practitioner

There are some personal qualities that will tend, on balance, to make your career in practice easier. These don't necessarily guarantee success, but they certainly help. What sorts of things characterize successful practitioners?

- *You like working with people.* Whether you're a technician or a manager, you'll be closely and continually involved with many different kinds of people throughout your career. If you don't much care for working with people, you're going to find it hard to succeed in practice, no matter how skilled you are.
- *You're adaptable.* You'll be asked to live, work, and even think

differently, at least part of the time. If you welcome the chance to be
flexible and to break with routine, you'll enjoy much of what you do
as a practitioner.

• *You're intellectually and socially curious.* If you look forward
to learning and trying new things, practice will present you with
plenty of opportunities.

• *You're tolerant and patient.* The ability to show perseverance
and patience in the face of frustrations and delays characterizes most
successful practitioners.

• *You're at ease with who you are.* As a practitioner, you'll need
to have a strong ego and a relatively thick skin. While you'll need to
flex and adapt in your work, it will help to have a strong inner core.

• *You have a sense of humor and proportion.* You can laugh at
yourself and at others when necessary. You have the ability to pull
back and take a break when things aren't working.

## Myths About Practice

There are many myths—positive and negative—about anthropological practice. The *positive myths* include these:

• *You make a lot of money.* It is sometimes true that you can
command a high salary or daily rate as a practitioner, but you
shouldn't count on it. In particular, be wary of comparisons between
academic salaries and your own. Just as most academics feel that
they could make more money outside the academy, so, too, do students. It's not necessarily true. Most new graduates have to seriously
revise their estimates of market worth.

• *Jobs are always challenging and interesting.* Not necessarily;
it depends very much on what you mean by "challenging and interesting." Sometimes you'll find yourself doing the most boring things
imaginable, but under very exotic circumstances.

• *A career in practice is personally satisfying and rewarding.* It
can be, but only if you make it so; it doesn't come automatically.
Practice—like any other line of work—will give you back only what
you put into it. Practice assignments are almost guaranteed to be
frustrating, at least part of the time, and your personal ability to turn
frustrations into rewards will be a crucial factor in your happiness
and satisfaction.

• *All you need is a degree in anthropology.* Most of this book is about what *else* you need in addition to anthropology in order to be a practitioner. Although anthropology is your core skill and your main world view, you need other skills and abilities to make your anthropology useful.

• *Everybody wants to hire anthropologists.* Although we've all seen the articles about anthropology as the "hot" new degree, don't expect people to come beating a path to your door. Most anthropology graduates still have to patiently explain to employers what they can do, how they work, and why they should be hired.

And then there are the *negative myths.* Some of the most common ones include these:

• *I'm turning my back on the discipline.* Not at all; you're carrying your discipline out into new areas, extending its reach and your own. You're not letting go of your anthropology; you're connecting it to something else.

• *I'm entering a den of thieves, where I'll lose any remaining shred of ethics and self-respect.* Although it may be hard to believe, the outside world is actually not such a bad place, and some would even say that it has less tolerance for rogues, charlatans, and uncivil behavior than the academy does. Although you'll find ethical challenges, you'll also find a high concern with ethics, and plenty of people with standards that you can admire.

• *I'm prostituting myself and peddling watered-down anthropology to people who wouldn't know quality if they tripped over it.* Hardly. As a practitioner, you'll learn what everyone learns: that ideas don't sell themselves, they need smart people to advocate for them. Few ideas in anthropology (or any other discipline, for that matter) will work straight out of the box, and that's what makes practice so fascinating. Because in the right hands, those ideas *will* work, and when they do, the folks around you will definitely take notice.

• *I'll never see my friends in the academy again.* Only if you choose not to reconnect. You're an anthropologist, and so are they. You have lots to talk about, and plenty of opportunity—through conferences, LPOs, and other venues—to do so. You can even teach a course once in a while, if you're so inclined.

• *It's going to be very lonely out there.* Not at all. There are thousands of anthropology practitioners in the workplace, and many more are on the way. LPOs and conferences, as noted, provide an excellent way for folks to get to know each other. The Internet, of course, makes it possible to talk about anything with anyone—anywhere, anytime. You may be the only anthropologist in your own workplace, but you're far from alone.

## The Future of Practice

The field of practice is certainly the major growth area within anthropology today, and arguably its most dynamic. The excitement and opportunity of anthropological practice have captured the interest and imagination of successive cohorts of graduates, with the result that there is now a large and increasingly well-organized practitioner community. Erve Chambers saw this clearly in 1985 when he wrote: "For the first time in the history of the profession, anthropology departments have begun to offer a clear professional role to people who want to involve themselves directly in the affairs of the world—individuals who are more motivated to take part in the actual processes of change than they are content to solely reflect upon the dynamics of social and cultural phenomena."[28]

The demand for this sort of anthropology is strong today, and it is likely to increase as the world becomes more interconnected. Meeting this demand will require the development of a corps of competent, articulate, and well-organized practitioners.

This effort is well under way. Practitioners are increasingly well organized, in ways which—although not exclusive of the academy— do not depend upon it. Although most published discussion of practice still occurs within the academy itself, university-based anthropologists no longer control the culture of practice taking shape beyond the campus. This would suggest that the future of practice— and possibly, the future of anthropology itself—may now lie outside the academy.

Not all would agree. Marietta Baba states: "Since practice is an extension of our discipline, one that depends on the base of the discipline for its sustenance, questions about the future of practice and its impact on anthropology as a whole ultimately must be addressed within academia."[29]

Leaving aside the question of whether or not practice *should* be shaped from within the academy (an issue on which I must disagree with Baba's position), I think that it is unlikely, as a practical matter, that it *will* be, unless and until the academy is prepared to restructure and reorient itself in some fundamental ways. And with each day that passes without these changes occurring, practice gains an increasingly independent presence in the world.

The culture and structure of the academy, for example, make it very difficult to maintain an engagement with issues outside the university on any full-time, sustained basis. For the same reasons, practitioners find it hard to participate fully in the training of students. And as tenure requirements become ever more rigorous, there is less incentive than ever before for young assistant professors to engage in anthropological practice, since they know that however valuable their contributions outside the academy might be, these will not count in decisions for tenure, promotion, and pay increases.

It is vitally important that this widening gulf between the academy and the world of practice be closed, if for no other reason than the fact that practitioners are in the process of developing a new kind of anthropology. Practitioners have grown increasingly sophisticated in developing effective means and methods for bringing anthropology to bear. They have been challenged, not just to put what they know to work, but to develop new skills and abilities.

As a result, they have much to teach their academic colleagues. Practice is not simply another kind of anthropology—it is a catalyst, providing an opportunity for the discipline to grow and change.

Let's turn now to the task of equipping you to enter this exciting world of practice.

## Notes

1. Bodley 1994: 352; Jean Schensul, *SfAA Newsletter* 7, no. 1 (1996): 2. Interestingly, no one really knows how many practitioners there actually are. A conservative estimate might be in the range of two to three thousand in the United States (see Fiske and Chambers 1996: 4, for example). This is conservative in the sense that it includes only those practitioners who have bothered to register themselves somewhere—e.g., with NAPA. There are probably thousands more, however, who possess advanced anthropology degrees—either the M.A. or the Ph.D.—and who are working outside the university. How many of these individuals still consider themselves to be anthropologists is an important question.

2. Montell 2000.

3. Van Willigen 1986: 34.

4. Bushnell 1976: 10.

5. Erve Chambers 1985: 214.

6. This formulation is similar to that used by Omohundro (1998: 31–32).

7. Schön (1983, 1987) has elaborated a framework for reflective practice. The knoll-and-swamp image comes from 1987: 3.

8. Schön 1987: 36, 157–158.

9. See Erve Chambers (1985: 175–176).

10. For more on learning from error, see David Korten's writings on the "learning process approach" to change; e.g., Korten (1980).

11. Material adapted from Schön (1983: 300); Brown (1984: 42).

12. Schön 1983: 129, 150–151.

13. Partridge 1979: 26, 1985; Honadle and van Sant 1985: 117. F. G. Bailey's books illustrate how meanings and outcomes are negotiated, on a multitude of levels. See, for example, Bailey (1969, 1983, 1988, 1991).

14. Johnsrud 2000: 98. See also Erve Chambers (1985: 221).

15. See van Willigen (1976: 88–90).

16. See Fiske and Chambers (1996: 1).

17. Hamilton 1973: 128–129.

18. Painter 2000: 79–80.

19. Singer 1994: 338.

20. Jenakovich and Murdock 1997: 18.

21. Price 2001a, 2001b. Price's findings are particularly interesting when compared with the 2000 National Doctoral Program Survey conducted by the National Association of Graduate and Professional Students (http://survey.nagps.org), which found, for anthropology graduate students, a relatively low level of satisfaction with their programs. Only 39 percent those surveyed responded positively to the statement "My program actively encourages students to explore a broad range of career options." Even fewer—28 percent—responded positively to the statement "My program does a good job of preparing students for careers outside of academia." See also the *Chronicle of Higher Education*, October 17, 2001.

22. See, for example, Grillo (1996) and Nolan (1998).

23. Drake 1988: 46–47.

24. Singer 1995: 46.

25. Drake 1988: 45.

26. Singer 2000.

27. Jenakovich and Murdock 1997: 17.

28. Erve Chambers 1985: 229.

29. Baba 1994: 179.

# 2

# PREPARATION
# FOR THE FIELD

This chapter outlines how someone who intends to be a practicing anthropologist should prepare for a career. The chapter begins by discussing the types of skills and collections of skills—called competencies—that practitioners must have. The chapter then looks at how students can use graduate programs in anthropology to acquire these competencies. We look first at the question of choosing an appropriate school and program, and then at how students can manage that program successfully. Three aspects of this receive particular attention: negotiating the elements of the academic program, choosing an academic adviser, and designing appropriate field experience.

## Skills for the World of Practice

In the future, few practitioners are likely to have *jobs* in the traditional sense of the term. Instead, they'll have a succession of *projects* that, although they may cluster around a specific topic or area, won't necessarily be connected. Think of authors or film directors: although there is certainly continuity in their work, what they do comes across as a series of projects—films and books—that are distinct creative products. But—and this is the point—in order to produce films or books at all, directors or writers must have specific abilities, which they apply to their undertakings, one after another.

So in this section of the chapter, we're going to talk about the skills you need to be a practitioner. We will look first at the basic qualifications that practitioners need, and then at how these combine into competencies.

## Threshold Qualifications

Threshold qualifications are aspects of your background that, although they will not guarantee you a job, will make you competitive in the marketplace. Threshold qualifications for anthropological practitioners fall into four main categories: academic training, language proficiency, field experience, and workplace skills.

*Academic training.* To be a fully fledged practitioner, you'll need a master's degree in applied anthropology (but see below if you want to stop with the B.A.). Later in the chapter, we'll look in detail at how to pick a graduate school, and how to design a program of study that meets your specific needs as an intending practitioner.

*Language proficiency.* Having a second language is increasingly necessary for a career in practice. There are nearly one hundred different languages used in schools in the United States alone, and many more out in the different communities that make up our increasingly multiethnic nation. And who's to say you won't want to work internationally in the future? No matter where you work or what you do, learning another language is an excellent way to develop a cross-cultural mind-set.

*Field experience.* You'll need to have some significant period of work in the field under your belt. Just because something was termed "field experience" in school doesn't necessarily mean that it adequately prepared you for practice. In a later section of this chapter, we'll look at several key components of what constitutes relevant field experience, and how you might acquire it.

*Workplace skills.* Workplace skills refer not to what you know, but to what you can do with what you know. In part, your workplace skills will be based on your academic preparation, but not entirely. The next section looks in more detail at workplace skills, and in particular, at those most relevant for practice.

## Workplace Skills

Academic preparation, language ability, and field experience are not skills in themselves, but indications that you may possess certain skills. Skills are not so much about knowing things, but about being able to do things with what you know. Having taken a course in methods, for example, doesn't necessarily mean that you are a good interviewer. Similarly, knowing the difference between *tu* and *vous* in French doesn't necessarily mean that you can use the correct form in a social situation.

Workplace skills are commonly divided into three basic categories: self-management skills, functional skills, and technical skills (see Table 2.1).

*Self-management skills.* Self-management skills are the basic attributes of an employable person: punctuality, neatness, sociability, politeness, etc. These things aren't normally taught in a university curriculum—you're expected to have them. Although these skills can be acquired, they are really based on your personal qualities: rather than having these skills, you *are* them. Employers will expect you to arrive with these and to use them intelligently. Few employers, obviously, are interested in training you to be on time for work, or to be considerate of others. In the professional world, these things are simply a given.

*Functional skills.* Functional skills, on the other hand, are those that help you do a job. They're similar in outline across a range of industries and occupations, although the way they're done in each may vary. Although functional skills deal with the concrete aspects of practice situation, they can be transferred from one job to the next. These skills arise partly from natural aptitudes—as with the ability to communicate, for example—but they are also learned through education and experience. It's your functional skills that can be most dramatically improved through training or experience.

*Technical skills.* Technical or job-related skills are highly specific to a particular field, profession, or situation. These skills are almost always rooted in a very particular context, and learned through special training or on-the-job experience. These skills are usually used to enhance and extend your functional skills. They are also the skills that you may lack if you're fresh out of school, or if your background is in another field entirely. Your anthropological training may give you some, but not all, of these skills. Employers will usually

**Table 2.1    Three Types of Skills**

| Technical Skills | Functional Skills | Self-Management Skills |
| --- | --- | --- |
| Programming in C++ | Writing a job description | Managing time |
| Speaking Swahili | Negotiating a business deal | Managing priorities |
| Coding a Federal Form SF-171 | Supervising another person | Communicating effectively |
| Piloting an aircraft | Planning a project | Managing conflict |
| Operating a shortwave radio | Running a meeting | Making decisions |
| Using a software package | Preparing a presentation | Flexibility |
| Designing a social survey | Writing a report | Tolerance |
| Outlining kinship structures | Drafting a budget | Cooperativeness |
| Diagnosing schistosomiasis | Writing a proposal | Punctuality |
|  | Editing a document | Reliability |

expect you to learn these on the job, and many organizations have training programs designed for that purpose.

As you prepare yourself for a career in practice, you are developing, in effect, three kinds of things: the kind of person you are (your *self-management skills*), your general ability to get things done (your *functional skills*), and your ability to work within a specific context or situation (your *technical skills*).

What combinations of skills are most useful for anthropological practice?

## Competencies for Anthropological Practice

Anthropologist practitioners need specific combinations of skills—which we'll refer to as competencies—to do their work. If you are intent on becoming a practitioner, therefore, you will need these competencies as part of your package of threshold qualifications (Table 2.2).

You probably already have some of these competencies, to one degree or another. If you need to add to your skills package or upgrade your skills, graduate programs exist that are tailored for intending practitioners. And even the more traditional anthropology graduate programs can be helpful in preparing you for practice, if you manage your time properly.

## What If You Only Want a B.A.?

Most of what's in this chapter is directed at people intending to enter a master's program. But what if you want to practice with just a B.A.?

**Table 2.2  Practice-Oriented Competencies**

| Competency | What This Does | Abilities or Skills Required | Some Typical Applications |
|---|---|---|---|
| Finding out things | Uncovering salient facts within a specific context; asking the right questions and being able to understand the answers. | Research design; interview techniques; literature and database search techniques. | Survey design; rapid assessment; literature review; interviewing; needs analysis. |
| Analyzing and learning things | Figuring out what the facts mean within the context; figuring out what results and outcomes teach us. | Statistics; content analysis; comparative research techniques; writing; tabular and graphic presentation techniques. | Data analysis; summaries; presentations; reports. |
| Communicating things | Telling others what we've learned; speaking and writing for different audiences. | Public-speaking skills; audiovisual presentation skills; graphic design skills; training design and delivery skills. | Presentations; reports; articles; briefings; monographs; training programs; advocacy sessions. |
| Planning and designing things | Knowing how to get things done within the context; keeping things moving smoothly. | Project and program design; proposal writing; budgeting; design of procedures; policy analysis and formulation. | Designing specific programs and projects; managing bureaucratic requirements; making policy. |
| Managing things | Being able to organize and sustain action toward established goals. | Decisionmaking; negotiation and conflict resolution; facilitation skills; job design; supervision; delegation; time planning and management. | Working with other people; assigning roles and responsibilities; troubleshooting and problem solving. |
| Judging things | Measuring accomplishment and assessing what the results mean. | Evaluation and monitoring design and methodologies; troubleshooting and modification. | Evaluating progress and outcomes; troubleshooting and problem solving; identifying success and failure. |

It is certainly possible, particularly if you have been fortunate enough to go through an undergraduate program that was applied in its focus. You may also have been able to arrange for a practice-oriented internship or field experience as part of your undergraduate program. And you may have access to practitioners in your area (through an LPO or other organization) who can help you find jobs.

If you've acquired a basic grounding in the practice competencies listed above, there's no real reason you can't start putting your anthropology to work as soon as you graduate. Anthropology is useful in hundreds of different fields, of course, and if you're interested in applying what you've learned, your job possibilities are only limited by your imagination.

There are some constraints, of course. As with anyone holding a bachelor's degree, you are well qualified for many jobs, but not for all. Once employed, you'll definitely be able to apply your anthropology, but often you'll be using your anthropology indirectly to support your primary activities in, say, marketing, communication, or community service. Your job description may not refer to anthropology at all. Some of the jobs that *do* have the word "anthropology" in them will probably require a master's degree.

Finally, you may eventually find that to advance in your work—whatever it is—you're going to need more specialized training. Fortunately, if you've already proven your worth to your organization, there's a good chance that you can get them to pick up some or all of the tab for more schooling. At that point, you may want to consider a master's, as a way not only of advancing professionally, but of making anthropology a central aspect of your work.

In this next section, therefore, we'll look at how to choose a graduate program, and later on, how to manage graduate school.

## Choosing a Graduate School

### What's Different About Graduate School?

In many ways, graduate school is designed as a rite of passage. You enter a kind of secret society, where you assume the identity of a postulant or neophyte. You are assigned a series of ritual tasks, one of the most important of which is the mastery of a body of sacred texts guarded by the tribal elders. Under their direction, you begin to study these texts; eventually, when you have convinced the elders that you have mastered their secrets, they pass you to the next level.

If you go straight from your senior year as an undergraduate into graduate school, you may experience a degree of status shock. You're no longer on top of the undergraduate hierarchy; you're a lowly graduate student, a sort of apprentice academic. Many if not most of your undergraduate friends will be gone, and chances are that your social life has all but disappeared.

But although you've got low status, you're still expected to toe the line. Unlike undergraduates, graduate students are considered to be part of the adult world on campus, and they are judged by professional standards. You'll also be considered a member—albeit a marginal one—of your department, and you'll need to play departmental politics carefully and skillfully. Indeed, you will become enmeshed in your department's affairs to an intense degree, whether or not the issues are directly relevant to what you are working on.

You will be expected to work on your own much of the time. You will have new responsibilities and be exploring new directions, often without much guidance or support from others. You will be expected to define and develop a specialty, to focus your energies primarily within that area, and to do an amazing amount of work, culminating in a dissertation or major project.

At the same time, you'll be in competition with others, both in your program and at other universities, for grants, fellowships, recognition, grades, placements, recommendations, and—ultimately—for jobs. The stakes are higher, the pressure is greater, and you'll probably feel overloaded at times. In addition to all that, your interpersonal relationships—with your adviser, your committee chair, and others—will now become much more professionally important to you.

More than anything, graduate school *counts*: the choices you make in graduate school—where to go, what to study, whom to study with—will have a marked effect on your career as a practitioner.

## Should You Get a Master's or a Ph.D.?

Given all this, you need to have your thoughts clearly organized before you begin graduate work. One of the most important of the initial decisions you will need to make is whether to opt for a master's degree or a Ph.D. If you want to be a practitioner, in other words, how much anthropology training is enough?

The Ph.D. is traditionally considered essential for a career as an academic. An extended period of fieldwork has been seen as an essential component of the Ph.D. experience. Obtaining a Ph.D. gives you advanced research skills and a deeper understanding of a specific area. It also signals to your colleagues that you have made a sincere commitment to a discipline. If you intend, now or ever, to become an academic, you *will* need a Ph.D., because without one you will not really be seen as someone who embraces academic culture.

To a growing degree, however, practitioners are graduates with a master's degree in anthropology. In some cases, these graduates have not had the time, money, or energy to pursue doctoral studies. In other cases—and increasingly, it would appear—they do not see the Ph.D. as terribly relevant for practice. To an increasing extent, anthropologist practitioners with the master's degree consider themselves sufficiently skilled for the demands of the workplace.

*Factors in the choice of degree.*   John Omohundro points out that there are three types of graduate programs in anthropology: programs that offer only the master's; programs that offer a master's as a terminal degree but also offer the Ph.D.; and programs that are primarily doctoral programs, but that award the master's as a sort of consolation prize if you don't manage to finish.[1]

Because many traditional programs of anthropological training assume that students will, if at all possible, obtain the Ph.D., this has posed problems for intending practitioners. A master's program will simply not have as much room within it for course work as a Ph.D. program, and so graduates may feel less well grounded in the fundamentals of anthropology. Less time may also be available for field experience. There are ways of overcoming these issues, however, as we'll see later in the chapter.

There are many reasons why students opt for a Ph.D., not all of them equally good. Better students, for example, often come under pressure from their teachers to pursue the Ph.D. In other cases, it is the undecided students who decide, *faute de mieux*, to go for the doctorate. Although the conventional wisdom says that advanced degrees mean better jobs and more money, it's not evident that anthropologist practitioners holding a master's degree are less well off than their Ph.D. colleagues.

Going for a Ph.D. instead of a master's must be looked at in terms of three things: time, money, and outlook. Time and money are connected, of course. A 1991 survey by the National Research Council showed that anthropology and sociology students were taking an average of 12.4 years from the B.A. to the doctorate, spending an average of just over 9 years actually registered as a student (and, one presumes, paying fees).[2]

Even if you're determined not to let it take this long, consider the fact that during the years you will spend in graduate school, you'll absorb an essentially academic world view. Although this will certainly serve you well if you enter the professorate, much of it may have to be unlearned if you are to succeed in the world of practice.

Often, anthropologist practitioners decide that their master's degree is quite sufficient for their professional needs. They network with other practitioners, and with colleagues within the academy, to stay abreast of trends and to learn new things.

Others, however, come to the conclusion that a Ph.D. is essential for particular kinds of work, either because the content of the doctorate is highly relevant to what they intend to do or (as is often the case) the degree itself is viewed by their colleagues as a necessary credential for admission into the inner circle.

And for some, a period of work following the M.A. leads to a decision to return to graduate school for a doctorate, either in anthropology or a cognate discipline, to enable them to work more effectively within their chosen field.

In the next section, we'll look at how one chooses a graduate program in anthropology. My assumption here is that you're choosing a master's program. Most of what is outlined below will apply equally well to Ph.D. programs, however.

## Training Programs for Practitioners

Fortunately, you have a fairly wide range of good schools to choose from. The first master's program in applied anthropology was begun in 1974 at the University of South Florida, and others followed suit. Field schools and internships (which we'll say more about later) are now a feature of the best applied programs.[3]

You don't absolutely need a degree from one of the applied or practice-oriented master's programs (see the Appendix for a list) to be a practitioner, of course, but it helps, for several reasons. First, the faculty are likely to have some experience with, and sympathy for, the practice option. Second, you'll probably find better resources for helping you with career choices. And finally, you'll find yourself in the company of like-minded student colleagues.

*Basic program elements.* NAPA's 1995 *Guidelines for Training Practicing Anthropologists* sets out some basic requirements for a good applied training program:

- The program should be named and offer a specialty.
- Responsibility for the program should be fixed, and that person should have a Ph.D.
- There should be an integrated, organized plan of study, and an identifiable body of students.
- There should be adequate funding for the program.[4]

NAPA also lists the elements of an adequate applied curriculum, which includes course work, mentoring, practical experience, and a thesis. Courses should include research methods, anthropological theory, relevant cognate areas, material on professional practice, and hands-on work.

Research on the Web will help you identify those schools that offer what you're interested in. Although there is no rating system in existence for these programs, you should also seek informed opinions from anthropology instructors, practitioners, students, and alumni.

*Planning site visits.* Once you've narrowed down your schools to a shortlist based on preliminary research, start looking at each one in detail. You should plan to visit each of the programs on your shortlist, and spend at least three or four days looking around and talking to people.

Because you know that your graduate school experience will have a transformative effect on you, take these site visits seriously. Focus on three main things during your site visit: the school and the area, the specific applied or practice program itself, and the anthropology department within which the program is housed. We'll take up each of these in turn in the sections below.

## Looking at the School

Although as a graduate student you may not actually have the time, energy, or inclination to interact much outside your own program, the university of which your program is a part is clearly important to you. You'll be spending years of your life—and many thousands of your hard-earned dollars—there.

*Can you get in?* Find out what the admissions requirements and procedures are. These may be set primarily by the individual department, but the university as a whole will also have admissions policies and criteria that also affect you.

One thing to keep in mind is that higher education is, in some respects, a buyer's market these days. All good graduate schools are very interested in attracting good students. If you have a good undergraduate record, you stand an excellent chance of getting into the school of your choice, particularly if you have taken the trouble to come to the campus and talk with department heads, program chairs, and admissions officers.

*What kind of a degree can you get?* Earlier, I mentioned that there were three basic types of anthropology graduate programs: master's only; Ph.D. with a fallback option to the master's; and master's programs with the Ph.D. as a later option. If you're intent on a Ph.D., then you obviously won't be considering the master's-only programs. Conversely, if you're set on the master's, you won't particularly care about a Ph.D. option. If you're undecided, however, it makes sense to ask some questions about how, in a program offering both degrees, one switches from one track to another.

The kind of university you attend will determine, to a marked degree, the kind of anthropology program you're likely to find there. "Elite" universities tend to have fairly traditional anthropology departments. They tend also to de-emphasize applied work, and train their students primarily for academic positions. It is the newer, or nonelite, schools, by and large, that have the applied programs, and where the emphasis may be more on training nonacademics.[5]

*What's the school like?* Some of the important factors related to the institution as a whole include these:

- *Tuition and cost of living.* Tuition rates for schools vary widely, of course. And so do cost-of-living levels in various places. You should think carefully about both of these things as you narrow your list of schools. Paying slightly more for tuition in one place may be more than offset by the lower cost of rent or groceries in that location.
- *Size and location.* East, West, or Midwest; North or South; big city or small town—these and other aspects of the location may be important to you. Location is not just geography, of course; it's environment (desert, mountains, plains, etc.), climate, and culture. It's also proximity to resources, opportunities, and activities. Many people feel quite at home in a large institution; others need a smaller community to feel a part of. Although larger institutions may have more resources, keep in mind that they'll also have more people making claims on those resources.
- *Reputation or ranking.* Consider these by all means, but don't take them too seriously. All of the various ranking systems for universities are flawed in one way or another, and schools themselves are quick to point this out (especially if they have not been ranked as they expected). There are no reliable ranking systems for anthropology departments, to say nothing of rankings for applied or practice-oriented programs, so you will just have to make up your own mind. And frankly, the ranking or reputation of your school really won't matter very much when you enter the world of practice. It's what you can do, not where you went to school, that counts.
- *Facilities and programs.* A good university library is an essential part of any graduate program. Bookstores, shops, classrooms, study carrels—these and other things will directly affect your life as a graduate student. If the school has joint degree programs, or a large number of extracurricular programs, this might also be an advantage.
- *Students.* We'll have more to say about the anthropology students in a moment. But here, let's focus on the university student body in general. Who are these people, where do they come from, and where are they going? Even though you may not interact with many of them while you're pursuing your graduate degree, you'll surely get involved with some of them.

To avoid feeling too much like a fish out of water later on, take a look at your fellow students now, before you commit. Some of them are likely to become your friends, or at the very least, your associates. Are they people you'd be interested in getting to know? Do many of them live on campus, or are most of them commuters? Are they older, married, working? What kinds of ethnic, national, or cultural diversity exist on campus? What kinds of extracurricular interests do these folks seem to have? What's the quality of life for students on this campus? How many of them graduate on time? How many drop out, and why?

## Looking at the Program

Look next at the specific program in applied or practicing anthropology. Most good programs are composed of similar elements. The core of the program will consist of a set of courses, usually emphasizing method and theory. Then there will be courses in one or more areas of specialization or concentration. There will usually be some opportunity to include courses from outside the program as well. There will be some arrangement for practice or application in the field. And finally, there will be some arrangement for integration and summation, often in the form of a thesis, examination, or final project.

**Figure 2.1   The Structure of a Typical Applied Program**

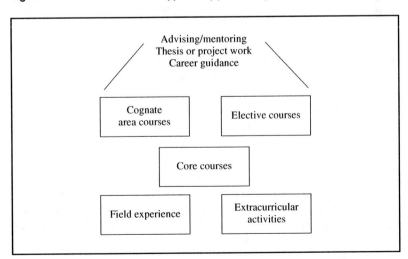

Within this basic structure, however, programs vary enormously, so it is very important for you to look closely at the details of each program on your shortlist.

What sorts of things should you be looking for? Here are some of the most important.

A *true applied emphasis.*   Pick a school that has predominant capability in the area you want. If you're interested in public health, for example, make sure the school you choose has a significant proportion of its resources (e.g., faculty, staff, books, courses) devoted to that field.

Look closely at the offerings, the instructors, and the overall philosophy of the program. How flexible is your program? To what extent can you design parts of your program yourself? Can you, for example, take courses in other departments that you feel you need but aren't in the program?

It shouldn't surprise you to learn that some programs are much more "applied" than others. Get course syllabi if possible, to see exactly what's being taught. Get faculty resumes if you can, and check for experience outside the academy. Look to see what type of field experience is required, and whether or not the program offers help in key professional areas such as career planning, job searching, and networking.

An *international and cross-cultural emphasis.*   Try to pick a school that emphasizes international and cross-cultural programs, activities, and linkages. The *Chronicle of Higher Education,* for example, publishes a yearly summary of the international activities of college campuses across the nation. For any specific school, you can easily find out, for example, how many of their students go overseas on study-abroad programs, how many international students there are on campus, and what special programs they may have on international or cross-cultural topics.

Why is this important? Because knowledge and technical skill aren't the only important things you'll learn in graduate school. You will also benefit from the context surrounding your training, and if that context reflects a wide diversity of cultures and viewpoints, you will gain a broader and more useful perspective on your future. Your fellow students will be more diverse, your teachers will have interests and experiences across cultures, and everything from student clubs to library holdings will reflect this.

*A solid track record in career development.* Any serious practice-oriented program will have a variety of ways to help students make good career choices. What does your program do specifically to help students with their nonacademic careers?

Look, for example, to see whether you can get specific guidance in professional networking, resume development and job searching, and interviewing skills. If these are available outside the department, that may be sufficient, but organized training run by anthropologists for anthropologists is the ideal. Are there career fairs or career resource centers in the department? Are nonacademic job opportunities regularly posted in the department?

Find out what the program knows about its past graduates. Do they keep track of them? How long does it take students to complete the program? How many students drop out of the program before completion, and why? How many get jobs in their chosen field? Do they have an active alumni network? If possible, you should arrange to talk with some of the program's recent graduates.

*The involvement of practitioners.* Students who intend to practice need to be exposed to different types of practitioners during their training. Practitioners can participate in training in a wide variety of ways: as adjunct professors, scholars-in-residence, visiting lecturers, project supervisors or advisers, etc. Ask program directors how practitioners are involved in their programs, and how this participation is planned and assessed.

*Substantial links outside the academy.* A program designed to prepare anthropology graduates for practice needs connections to the outside if it is to remain current and relevant. Links between academic programs and the outside can be of many different types: e.g., joint projects, internships, and representation on boards, committees, and other outside bodies. Find out what these links are, and what substantive activities take place through them. Find out also if the links are current and active, and how many faculty are involved.

*Externally based performance criteria.* A program to prepare professionals ought to be able to describe, precisely and in detail, how it measures success among those it graduates. These evaluative criteria ought to reflect external realities rather than the subjective judgments of faculty alone. How, specifically, does the program do this, and how successful is it?

## Looking at the Department

Finally, don't forget to look at the larger anthropology department of which your program is a part.

*Faculty.* You're not just picking a program, you're picking teachers to work with. These people will guide you, teach you, and challenge you. Ultimately, they will have a considerable influence over the direction your career—and your life—takes.

Look first at the applied and practice-oriented faculty. Who are they? What is their background and training? What are their specific interests? Are they likely to be interested in you? What are they doing research on, and how does this fit with your interests? Are they accessible and willing to spend time with students? Are they good teachers? How much time do they actually spend teaching?

Make sure that there is at least one person on the faculty that you would be happy to have as an adviser or mentor. Try to meet at least once with this person during your visit. Find out, if you can, if this person might be willing to work with you, should you choose to join the program.

*Students.* How many students are in the applied program? How many students are in nonapplied programs? How different from the applied students are they?

Why did the current students choose to come here? How do they describe themselves? What are they interested in, both inside and outside the program? What career aspirations do these students have? Are they a diverse group, or do they tend toward a common set of characteristics? Do they seem to have good relationships with faculty? With each other?

*Resources.* What resources does the department have, and specifically, what is available for your program? Do they have special libraries, workrooms, or other educational resources? Unless the entire department is an applied one, your program will be competing for resources, financial and intellectual, with other programs in the department.

Is the department bringing in enough money to be able to fund you or to support you for conferences, internships, etc? Are there part-time teaching or work opportunities available through the department? What other forms of financial aid do they have?

In addition to an applied or practice program, what other options are available for students? Are these considered more important than the applied offerings? Where are most of the students and faculty concentrated? Do the department's offerings connect with one another, or are they largely separate? How much do the various faculty members actually know about the other options?

*Departmental climate.*   Every department will have a climate or feel all its own. This will be shaped by both external and internal forces.

How is the department considered on the campus as a whole? The reputation of a particular department (or program) on its own campus has a direct effect upon you as a student. Departments that are seen, for whatever reason, as marginal to the interests of the university as a whole are often subjected to budget cuts and other unpleasantries, all of which will roll down to students in one way or another.

Internally, does the department get along with itself? How do the applied faculty get along with the nonapplied faculty? Is there a collective intellectual life, expressed through seminars, symposia, etc.? If there are major factions or divisive issues within the department, you can be certain that you will be drawn into these, one way or another. How do the faculty get along with their support staff (e.g., the secretaries, research assistants, etc.)? If the support staff feel overburdened, you can be sure, once again, that you will eventually bear the brunt of their discontent.

Just as you'll need to manage your career as a practitioner, you'll also need to manage your career as a graduate student. Three aspects of this are particularly important, and we'll focus on them in the remaining sections of this chapter.

One is that of negotiating a specific program of study within the confines of the overall program you've chosen. The second is choosing an appropriate adviser to work with as you go through the program. And the third is that of setting up the right kind of field experience to complement your classroom experiences.

We'll take these up now, one by one.


## Negotiating a Program of Study

You will get the most out of a graduate program if you come into it with a clear sense of what your present skills are, what new skills you want to acquire, and an agenda for using what you expect to learn.

## Core and Periphery

Most programs of applied anthropology have a similar basic structure, as outlined earlier. You will presumably be familiar by now with the outlines of your program: the core requirements, the specialization options, the field experiences, and the integrative activities, such as a project or thesis. You will not be able to change these very much, but you should sit down with your adviser early in your program, to look in detail at the content of your program, and to determine how it matches with your personal and professional needs.

Begin by looking at areas within the program where you have choices. Move out from that to include cognate areas—not necessarily included within your program—that may be important for you as a practitioner. Keep John van Willigen's advice in mind. He cautions that "you will not be hired on the basis of your being the best anthropologist; they [employers] must see you as a skills-possessing problem solver that relates to their organizations' need to be more efficient, more sensitive, more effective, more responsive, or more profitable."[6] You will be hired, in other words, for what you can do, not for what you have studied. You should therefore choose courses and activities that provide you with the opportunity to build skills for practice, whether they lie within anthropology itself or in related areas: for example, management, public administration, and international studies, just to name a few.

You should be aware of major gaps in your preparation, and you should design your program to help fill those gaps. As you put your program together, you should also have a fairly clear idea of what your concentration or specialty will be. Finally, you should also have specific ideas about what you might want to do your research project or thesis on. In this way, you'll avoid getting sidetracked, for example, into your adviser's main interest.

## Using Learning Contracts

It's possible that your anthropology program will provide top-notch training in all of the professional competencies outlined earlier in this chapter. Possible, but unlikely. Although much of your program will be prescribed for you, important parts of it will be relatively open and flexible, under your personal control. It will be up to you, in other words, to manage your learning in these areas, and it is here that you can play a major role in shaping not only what you learn, but how you learn it.

One effective way to do this is to draw up a *learning contract* with your adviser at the beginning of your program. A learning contract is a written agreement between you and your adviser that outlines a plan for reaching specific educational goals. The learning contract can be broad—covering your entire degree program—or it can be relatively narrow—focusing, for example, on your internship or field experience.

Such contracts put learners rather than instructors at the center of the learning process, and give them a great deal of responsibility and input. As an individual, you have a learning style all your own, and you may find that a learning contract helps you learn more effectively. Drafting a learning contract is your responsibility, not your adviser's. Your adviser is there to help you and guide you, but not to lead you.

A learning contract will allow you to be specific about what you personally want to learn and how. It will encourage you to find creative ways of learning these things. It will ensure that the results of your learning are both tangible and explicit. And finally, it will make you and your adviser personally accountable for the results achieved.[7]

To create a learning contract, you'll need to consider four main questions:

- Learning Objectives: What do you want to learn and why?
- Strategies, Resources, and Activities: How will you learn it?
- Products to Be Assessed: What will the results look like?
- Assessment Criteria and Procedures: How will the results be judged?

Learning contracts are highly individualized, specific, and outcomes-oriented. Done properly, a learning contract will motivate both you and your adviser to make the most of your time in the program. Although the contract is written, it is flexible and can be changed as circumstances warrant. A series of learning contracts, in fact, can chart your progress through the program.

## Learning Outside the Program

There's a great deal that you can do to build your skills while in school, other than just attending classes. If you've chosen wisely, your school will have opportunities for you outside the program itself. Take advantage of as many of these outside resources and opportunities as you can.

*Career counseling.*   Even if your own department doesn't provide all of the career support you'd like, this may be available from some other office on campus. Find the people in your school whose job it is to help graduates with their career choices. Talk with them and follow up the leads they provide, so that you are as well informed as possible by the time you get your degree.

Many schools provide university-wide workshops on a variety of aspects of job hunting and career planning, including training in such things as interviewing, networking, resume writing, etc. They may also arrange career days or job fairs, or some other form of structured introduction to the world of work.

Find faculty in other departments who've had experience outside the academy in areas of interest to you. Start talking with them and asking for advice. Don't rely on one faculty mentor or adviser alone; try to triangulate the advice you get by comparing it with other sources.

*Professional conferences.*   Plan to attend as many professional conferences as you can while you are a graduate student. Conferences are an excellent place to observe professional debates and discussions, and even participate in some of them. You will also have the opportunity to learn about the latest controversies, hot topics, and opportunities. Presenting a paper at these conferences, and serving on a panel, are excellent ways of polishing your professional skills, while at the same time bringing yourself—and your work—to the attention of others outside your program.

Conferences, of course, are an excellent way to network and make contacts. Because conferences are usually held in major cities, this is also a chance to network with various agencies and organizations with which you might want to work later on.

Get organized in advance for conferences. Your adviser can help you with introductions and advice. Take copies of your resume and copies of some of your work. If you'll be interviewing, learn about the organizations in advance.

*Consulting and research opportunities.* If you are lucky enough to be in a department that is involved in outside projects, get connected with these if at all possible. This will give you an excellent introduction to the world of contracting and consulting. You may be able to complete a piece of the project on your own, or you may have a chance to work with—and learn from—a respected senior faculty member. Consulting is, by and large, more valuable to you than straight research, although both are useful for building your skills.

*Professional writing.* Since so much of the world of practice—in virtually any sphere—is tied to reports and proposals of various kinds, developing the ability to do these is excellent preparation for your career. Most faculty members will be delighted, in fact, to accept your offer to help them put together grant proposals or reports. In the process, you'll gain insight into how to present results and recommendations effectively, how to shape your writing to different audiences, and—above all—how to write clearly and succinctly.

*Language acquisition.* Earlier, we said that knowing another language was a key threshold qualification for practice. There are several reasons why this is so.

If you intend to work domestically, you will eventually encounter situations in which skill in another language will become important. Our developing trade relationships with Mexico and Canada alone will ensure this. In addition, the rapid growth of non-Hispanic immigration is creating large communities of people who speak every imaginable language on earth, and who connect in various ways with a wide range of government and nonprofit agencies.

If you intend to work internationally, of course, language proficiency is also a must. In the international-development sphere, for example, five main working languages dominate: French, English, Spanish, Arabic, and Portuguese. In addition, there are a number of other languages widely spoken across national boundaries, such as Hindi, Turkish, Russian, Indonesian, Hausa, and Swahili.

Learning any language at all is highly desirable, for the simple reason that it gives you a window into other ways of seeing and thinking. This ability to enter into the lives of others is a very valuable skill, and will distinguish you from the thousands of other job seekers who cannot do this.

## Managing Graduate School

For most of your instructors, the academy is a total institution. Many of them know no other life; some of them can imagine no other life.

You, however, are a sojourner: a transient outsider raiding the temple of knowledge for useful material. You get in, fill your sack, and when it's full, it's time to leave. You came to graduate school because you wanted to practice anthropology on the outside. As pleasant as the university might be, it's not where you'll be spending your professional life, so as soon as you're ready, you should go. After all, you can always come back.

*Getting started early.*   Begin thinking about your thesis right away, and work on it throughout. Decide on the topic as early as possible, and make your papers and other assignments dovetail with this topic in one way or another, by developing aspects of it, exploring options, describing research techniques, examining concepts and literature, etc. Begin, in other words, with the end in mind.

*Managing your time.*   If you developed bad time management habits as an undergraduate, lose them now, and fast. They will only cause you grief. Stay efficient and organized. Keep control of your time; don't procrastinate.

*Prioritizing.*   You can't take advantage of everything offered by your school, and it's easy to get overcommitted. Always have a plan for what you're doing. Keep your goals in mind, and stick to a realistic timetable for accomplishments. Review goals and priorities regularly, and adjust where necessary. If you are constantly falling behind, revise your schedule. A learning contract may help keep you on track.

*Not working yourself to death.*   Balance your life and your work. Although our culture assigns these to separate categories, life and work are just aspects of the same thing, and they need to be in harmony. So take time off when you need to, while not losing sight of your goals.

*Managing your thinking.* Graduate school can challenge your self-respect and confidence, at least at first. You will no doubt experience frustrations and delays, and even stupidity from time to time. Stay centered, and don't take things too personally. Smile, be gently persistent, and make a little headway every day.

*Contributing.* Find useful things to do. Try to stay busy throughout your graduate program with something outside the classroom—a job, a volunteer assignment, or some other form of activity that engages you with the world beyond the academy, and through which you make a valued contribution to some group enterprise.

*Making everything count.* You have limited amounts of time, energy, and money: don't waste them. If you're going to spend time taking courses, for example, make sure that each and every one of them will help you become a better practitioner. In the courses themselves, if you have to write long analytical papers, then make sure you choose a practice-related topic to write on. If you're required to do data analysis, use the assignment to learn a new statistical procedure or a new software program.

*Talking to people and learning from them.* You're surrounded by intellect and experience, so take advantage of it. Everyone knows something. Talk regularly with your adviser, other members of the faculty, faculty in other departments, and your fellow students. Think of yourself as doing fieldwork, if it helps. If you're getting advice that you're not sure of, seek other opinions. Never lose an opportunity to learn something more.

## Choosing an Adviser

The choice of your adviser is probably the most important single decision you will make in graduate school. In many ways, this person will be instrumental in helping you prepare for your career. An adviser is a type of mentor, and as we'll see in a later chapter, mentors are a very important professional resource for you. Some people recommend that you base your choice of graduate program primarily on the question of who your adviser will be; that you choose the adviser rather than the program.

In many ways, this makes sense. It's often difficult, however, to size up an adviser during the course of a campus visit, and so you may not be able to choose an adviser—and have her choose you—before you decide on a program. But at least be sure that, within a given program, you have some acceptable choices from among the faculty.

## How Your Adviser Can Help You

A good adviser can be enormously helpful to you in school. To begin with, your adviser will be able to provide you with an orientation to your new environment. After you settle in, your adviser will continue to be a kind of cultural informant, telling you things you need to know about where you are, what lies ahead, and how to make smart choices.

Your adviser can offer you many things: insight, wisdom, perspective, and the benefits of hard-won experience. She will be able to help you thread the academic bureaucracy, and can tell you whom to see to get what you need. Your adviser will be able to give you honest feedback and criticism, and will instruct you in the standards of professional performance.

Advisers can also provide you with contacts outside the university, and possibly with career opportunities. If you are fortunate enough to have an adviser who has been involved in anthropological practice, then her nonacademic experience will be invaluable to you.

## Making the Choice

Your graduate school adviser should be someone who cares about you and your future, is willing to help you, and, at times, to challenge and push you. You want support from your adviser, but you also want honesty.

Your adviser should be accomplished, enthusiastic, experienced, a good manager and teacher, and have a good reputation with students and a compatible personality. She should be a mature professional (ideally with tenure), still energetic and enthusiastic. Although there's always the chance that your adviser will take a job at another university halfway through your program, try to pick someone who seems settled and comfortable.

Does your adviser's academic reputation matter? If you are intending to stay in academia, then, yes, it matters quite a bit. Wherever you go in later years, you will be "so-and-so's student." Outside academia, however, few people may have heard of your adviser, or even of your department. They will be more likely to have heard of your university.

Different advisers have different styles, and the question of personal fit and chemistry is all-important. Some advisers behave more like collaborators, and like to work closely with you. Others are hands-off, offering only occasional bits of advice. Whatever her style, your adviser should have clear, high standards, reasonable and consistent expectations of her students, and respect for their needs.

Tap other students' experiences with different members of faculty as you search for an adviser. For a particular individual, find out things like: Does she give her advisees enough time? Do her students finish quickly? Does she give them credit for their work? Do other students respect her? Do her students get good jobs?

Keep in mind that your adviser has a stake in your performance, just as you do in hers. Should you fail or mess up, your adviser will be tainted to a degree. This is known as the "black halo" effect.[8]

Finally, don't let the relationship get out of hand. It's supposed to be helpful, not overwhelming. Occasionally, advisers wind up acting like either Svengali or Pygmalion. Neither of these models, obviously, is a healthy one.

## Gaining Field Experience

### Types of Field Experience

Anthropologists—both academics and practitioners—are in a sense defined and created by their field experience. The field is where many key workplace skills are acquired and practiced.

There are many models of field experience, other than the classical lone-wolf model, where an individual spends a long period of time in an exotic and faraway locale. Although this might be fun, you probably won't have time during a master's program, and in any case, the lone-wolf model won't do much to train you for practice.

Table 2.3 sets out some of the alternatives. Although all of these differ in some important respects, all of them are opportunities for you to learn outside the confines of the classroom.

As you think about field experience, you should keep several considerations in mind. They include:

- Timing: When does the experience take place, and how long does it last?
- Type of Assignment: Where will you be assigned? Will you be alone or with others? Will this assignment be paid or unpaid? What sorts of things will you do? Who decides these?
- Supervision and Evaluation: Who will be supervising you during this time? How will you be evaluated, and by whom? Will your academic adviser be involved?
- Credit: Will you get academic credit for what you do? How will this be decided?
- Documentation and Outcomes: What will be produced at the end? Will you need to do a report or a project?

If you have field experience built into your program, well and good. If not, you can—and should—design your own field experience. Field experiences are unparalleled opportunities to build skills in the real world, in the context of place, people, and project. The experience will take you far beyond what could be achieved in the classroom alone. Taking extra time for field experience may delay your progress toward the degree somewhat, but it will be more than worth it in terms of professional preparation.

## The Benefits of Field Experience

The benefits of field experience are numerous. The most important benefit is that of application. Field experience allows you to apply or practice what you have learned in the classroom, but under real-world conditions. Your understanding of the link between theory and practice is thereby deepened.

You can use field experience to fill in gaps in your academic training, or to extend and expand skills you already have into new areas. At the same time, you will learn new and sometimes unexpected things.

Field experiences provide information about possible careers: you can explore an industry or sector, and learn about specific

**Table 2.3    Types of Field Experience for Practitioners**

| | |
|---|---|
| Volunteer | As the name implies, this is unpaid. Volunteer assignments are usually individual, and take place during vacation periods, or part-time in evenings and on weekends during school. Work assignments vary widely, as does the duration of the assignment, which is usually not supervised by an academic adviser. Academic credit is usually not given for volunteer assignments. May or may not involve some formal method of evaluation and write-up. |
| Field school | Field schools are usually arranged as academic experiences that take place "in the field"—i.e., somewhere outside the university, often in a foreign country. Students go as a group, and are accompanied by faculty members. The experience is generally oriented around research, and is often structured as a way to help students acquire and practice research methodologies. The field school is unpaid; indeed, students must usually pay tuition and other costs in order to attend. Field schools are typically timed to fit with the academic calendar, and will last for 2–8 weeks during the summer, or for an academic term or quarter. Students are closely supervised, evaluated by faculty, and given academic credit for their work. The work is generally well documented. |
| Service learning | Service-learning programs are growing in popularity on U.S. campuses. Students receive academic credit for participating in projects and programs run by organizations outside the university, often community nonprofits. Assignments vary widely. Students may work individually or in groups. They are generally supervised closely within the organization, and they may also be supervised by people from the university. Assignments are generally unpaid. Students are evaluated, and some documentation of their experience is usually required. Service-learning programs are geared to the demands of the academic calendar. |
| Internship | "Internship" is a general term denoting a temporary assignment in an organization. Students often arrange these themselves, or through a university unit. Assignments and the duration of assignments vary widely. Academic credit may or may not be given. Internships may be paid or unpaid; if paid, they are unlikely to be highly paid. The degree of supervision of an internship will vary considerably, as will the involvement of academic advisers in the experience. Evaluation may or may not take place, and the amount of actual documentation required may range from none to extensive. |
| Practicum | Practicums are supervised opportunities for students to use the skills they have acquired in the classroom by applying them to a real-world problem. A practicum may take place outside the university, or, in some cases, it may not be necessary for students to leave the classroom (e.g., for certain types of design or consulting problems). The practicum may consist of one problem or many. Academic credit is generally given, and the involvement of advisers is usually extensive. The practicum experience is generally not paid, but is an integral part of the academic program. Practicums are geared to the academic calendar, and may occur more than once in the course of a program, depending on their duration. Practicums can involve individual students or students working in groups. Students are evaluated, and documentation tends to be extensive. A project or final product is often the outcome of a practicum. |
| Cooperative assignment | Cooperative education programs are a feature of a number of U.S. professional schools. These involve alternating terms in the classroom with terms in the workplace, according to a tightly planned schedule. Work assignments are often paid, and often at relatively high levels. The students are expected to take on assignments in the workplace that are close to what ordinary employees do. They are supervised from within the company or organization, and also evaluated by academic advisers. Assignments vary considerably, but tend to be highly professional in nature. A typical co-op school will usually require its students to undertake more than one co-op placement during the program. The duration of co-op periods varies, but they are generally scheduled for an entire term at a time and keyed to the academic calendar. |

industry practices and requirements. You will operate within a setting, organization, or project where you will be able to measure your own skills and abilities against those already working full-time.

You will be required to work with others. You'll normally have a supervisor, and so the field experience will help you learn how to communicate with, and work with, a boss. You'll also have colleagues and co-workers. You'll learn how to get along with them, through the experience of working together on group projects.

Your field experiences will give you valuable networking contacts. If your field experience is with an organization where you might like to work someday, the time you spend with them as a student is a useful no-risk period for everyone, to allow you to get acquainted. Field experience is especially helpful for opening doors in highly competitive fields, or in ones where your own qualifications aren't well understood.

During your field experiences, you'll be shifting gears, moving into a more proactive role in learning. You're away from school, more in charge of your situation, and more responsible for what happens. You're engaged in meaningful and useful work, applying your learning and judging the results. Most students gain both motivation and self-confidence from field experiences, and they return to the classroom reenergized.

## Differences Between the Field and the Classroom

Because the students in a field situation are really apprentice-practitioners, they learn as practitioners do. This requires students—and their teachers—to approach the field situation differently from the classroom.

In the field, you'll be an active rather than a passive learner. The goals and activities of the field experience should be those set by the student, or jointly by the student and the teacher/supervisor, rather than simply being assigned. If your faculty members are involved in the field experience with you, they'll probably play a much less directive role there than they do in the classroom, serving more as coaches than experts.

The content of what is learned depends a great deal on the situation itself, rather than being dictated by theory or abstract models. The methods of learning tend to be collaborative and group-based, rather than individual and competitive. Finally, the outcomes of the experience tend to be assessed by the students themselves, according to standards of their own choosing, rather than according to some outside measure.

## Designing the Field Experience

Field experiences work best when they are well designed. Your adviser should be closely involved in the design, whether or not she is involved in the experience itself. Ideally, people in the organization, agency, or situation you will be entering will also be involved in the design. The activities you are planning should be useful to them in some direct way, just as the outcomes you seek should be useful to you within the context of your academic program. There should be a clear set of guidelines or ground rules that all of you have agreed on, as well as opportunities for feedback.[9]

Begin by brainstorming with your adviser the kinds of field experiences you'd find most useful. Then start looking at likely organizations and situations. Once you've found what you want, identify a person in the field who will be your supervisor.

Whatever the form, content, or location of your field experience, you should seek to include these key components:

• *Work in organizations:* for practitioners, it's important to have an understanding from the inside of how organizations operate. Working in an organization will therefore be much more valuable than working on your own.

• *Work on a project:* a project is an organized activity, temporary in nature, containing a clear set of objectives or outcomes. If at all possible, get involved with a project. It will give you an excellent sense of the design choices practitioners make, and how they work under deadlines.

• *Application:* try by all means to involve yourself with something that will let you practice what you've learned. You'll certainly be learning new things, but you should also seek opportunities to use what you already know.

• *Work with others:* even within an organization, it's possible to work all by yourself. Avoid doing so. As a practitioner, you'll need to have teamwork skills, and the way to acquire and refine them is to work with others.

Make a plan—ideally, centered around a learning contract—and discuss it with both your instructor and your supervisor. Defining your own learning objectives clearly will help you communicate these to others, and will increase your chances of having a productive experience.

You may need to make formal application to the organization for your experience. If so, write and tell them about yourself and your learning needs. Be as specific as possible. Be prepared to be flexible, but tell them what you're hoping to be able to do, how much time you can devote to them, and what special skills or abilities you have. Tell them not only how you think you can benefit their organization by working for them, but also about how what you hope to learn relates to your studies.

## An Opportunity to Learn to Think Differently

Ideally, your field experience should involve significant time spent in an other-cultural environment. The out-of-culture aspect is important for many reasons. In addition to giving you a chance to practice your information-gathering and analysis skills, working in another culture will make you more aware of yourself as a culturally based professional. Like language study, work in cross-cultural situations allows you to learn how to see and think using different frameworks.

You don't necessarily need to go overseas to get cross-cultural experience. Any situation that takes you out of your own zone of familiarity will do, as long as you are prepared to learn from it. Some of the important characteristics of a cross-cultural experience include these:

- Having to operate in a new or different frame of reference: using another language; learning new technical procedures.
- Working in an unfamiliar environment: working away from home, in a new industry, with new kinds of people.
- Working with people of a different background: working with senior citizens, children, hospital patients, or people from a different ethnic or cultural group.
- Working with people who have a different value system: working across lines of ethnicity, gender, socioeconomic class, or occupation.

- Working in a situation where two different value systems intersect: working in a relief agency, community outreach organization, social service agency, police force, etc.
- Working in a situation of scarce resources: working for a nonprofit group, charity organization, student group, etc.
- Working in situations of ambiguity and/or uncertainty: working for a political cause or campaign.
- Needing to be flexible in what you do: working with community groups or on highly charged issues.
- Needing to learn in an uncertain environment or under pressure: research projects in unfamiliar areas; emergency response teams.

An optimal field experience would take place in a setting that closely approximates a situation of practice, but which allows students a chance to experiment at low risk, to take "time out," and to discuss and analyze what is happening. Through engagement and dialogue, students would build up an understanding of how the practice situation is constructed, how it operates, and—finally—how to work within it. Students would have opportunities to demonstrate competence in some of the key activities that they will be expected to perform as professionals.

What might some of these be? Donald Schön suggests the following:

- Taking "dirty" data and making sense of them
- Writing clearly about complex issues
- Dealing with people who see the world differently in a way that gets things done
- Working through difficult political and interpersonal issues while still keeping hold of the important ideas
- Dealing with people who disagree with you in a positive and productive way[10]

## Managing the Field Experience

Typically, you'll enter a field situation where you're the inexperienced newcomer. Most of the folks around you will know more than you do, at least at first. Think about how to learn most effectively in that type of situation. Try to get teamed with someone who knows more than you do about something you'd like to learn about, and who has the time and willingness to teach you some of it.

Field experience gives you a chance to try your hand at different things. You should extend yourself as much as possible, learning about different aspects of the job or situation. Don't ask whether what you're doing is "real" anthropology or not. Ask instead: How can I use anthropology to perform this task or to solve this problem?

In your field experience, you may be assigned different roles. In some situations, you may be primarily an observer. In others, you will be assigned one job—or one project—and be expected to stick to it for the duration of your time there. Sometimes you will rotate through a set of activities or projects, filling in where needed. In still other situations, you may be "apprenticed" to an older professional, and expected to work closely with that person and learn from him or her.

Don't expect your field experience to be a smooth ride from start to finish. As with cross-cultural sojourns, you'll probably go through an initial honeymoon period followed by some disillusionment as workplace realities sink in. As with any field situation, you'll face a steep learning curve. But as you gain familiarity with your new situation, your confidence and competence will grow.

Try to keep a journal of some kind during your field experience, so that you can draw on it later. Journal writing will help keep you attentive to both your surroundings and what you are learning from your surroundings. Later, you can mine your journal for insights that can be incorporated into your professional portfolio (discussed in Chapter 4). Your journal can also help you understand and communicate to others the value added by your field experience.

Finally, good field experiences should involve participants in several different types of follow-up activities. Telling others about your experience, for example, allows you to share information and insights. Analyzing the field situation—in a paper or report, for example—allows you and your fellow students to see similarities and differences, comparisons and contrasts, across a range of locales. Discussing the experience with your adviser or supervisor involves you in being self-critical about how well you—and they—were able to meet the demands of the situation.

Follow-up ensures that the value added from experience is identified, discussed, and shared, both for the benefit of the current cohort of students and—for teachers—in order to design the next generation of learning situations.

## Notes

1. Omohundro 1998: 42–43.
2. In Peters (1992).
3. Trotter (1988) provides an excellent introduction to the structure, content, and philosophy of these applied training programs. See also Hyland and Kirkpatrick (1989).
4. On the ANTHAP website (http://anthap.oakland.edu).
5. See Price (2001a and b) and Shankman and Ehlers (2000).
6. Van Willigen 1986: 213.
7. See Anderson, Boud, and Sampson (1996) for a helpful discussion of learning contracts and how to construct them.
8. Zey 1984: 137.
9. See Angrosino (1981) for more discussion.
10. See Schön (1987: 17, 158–162, 303, and 333–334) for an extended discussion of the practicum as a way to train practitioners.

# 3

# CAREER PLANNING

C hapter 3 takes up the task of planning a career as an anthropological practitioner, beginning while you are in graduate school. The chapter first presents an overall strategy for career planning and job hunting, details of which will be covered in this and the following chapter. The overall shape of the nonacademic job market is briefly outlined, as is the role of interests, values, and skills in determining career choices. The chapter then looks in detail at the types of skills that anthropology graduates bring to the market, and how these compare with the skills of other graduates. This is followed by a section on information gathering, using both networking and informational interviewing, as a very important step in career planning. These two techniques—based on skills that anthropology graduates are already familiar with—will enable graduates to investigate and choose among different career options before they begin a formal job search.

## Planning Your Career

While the last chapter focused on qualifications, this one will focus on developing your career strategy. A clear career strategy, coupled with strong qualifications, will get you a job as a practitioner.

Start planning your career strategy as soon as you enter graduate school: the process of defining what you want to do and why is empowering, and will have a positive effect on your studies.

In the early stages of planning, as you are collecting information and relating it to your professional goals, you will learn more about yourself, and about the connection between what you know, what you want, and what is available to you in the workplace. It's a lot like fieldwork, where every conversation, interview, or observation gives you a fresh set of clues, a better set of questions, and a little more insight into what's going on around you. The process of defining your career will take time, thought, and energy, but it will also prepare you for job hunting, and will help ensure your success.

## Steps in Career Planning

There are several fairly simple steps to planning your career as a practitioner.

The first step is *visioning*—trying to imagine your ideal job situation. This is not fantasy, but a realistic image of the future arising out of your values, your skills, and your interests.

The second step involves collecting information about the kinds of possibilities or options that fit with your vision. You do this in two main ways: through *networking* and *informational interviewing.*

Once you have collected sufficient information, you will move to the third step, and perform a simple *SWOT analysis*. This will match your strengths and weaknesses to the opportunities and threats in the external job market. The purpose of the SWOT analysis is to

**Figure 3.1　An Outline of Your Job Search Stategy**

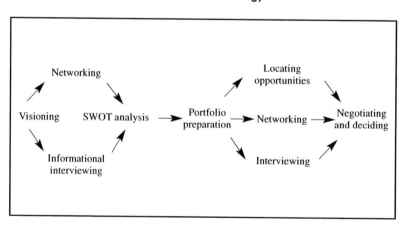

allow you to identify your specific comparative advantage, prior to starting your job search.

We'll take up visioning, information collection, and SWOT in this chapter. Chapter 4 will look at how you can use the results of SWOT to construct a professional portfolio, and how to use your portfolio in a job search.

This approach to career planning and job hunting has a number of specific advantages for graduate students. First, it allows you to ease into the process by focusing initially on your own interests, values, and skills, and then on information gathering. This gives you the opportunity to learn new things and adjust your goals and actions accordingly, before you actually begin a job search.

Second, this approach is highly weighted toward networking— that is, toward personal contacts—as a way to gather information and evaluate options. Lists, ads, and websites can provide a great deal of information, but in the end, it is your personal, face-to-face interactions that will enable you to make the right choices.

Third, the strategy delays preparation of your resume until you have thoroughly explored likely employment possibilities. In this way, you will be able to prepare a portfolio that is targeted, persuasive, and professional.

The decisions you make as you work your way through this process will be important ones, in that they will both guide and constrain your future choices and possibilities. But they are not irrevocable. You will be able to change course as you go, based on what you are learning.

In many respects, career planning is like a sailboat race. You need to have a clear sense of the ultimate goal or destination, but along the way you will make frequent changes of course and adjustments to your sails to take account of winds, currents, and other shifting factors.

## Visioning

### The Job Market for Practitioners

*Key characteristics.* One of the reasons for starting your planning early is that the market for practitioners is quite different from that for academic anthropologists. It differs in several important ways.

For one thing, it is not really structured. Whereas academic jobs fall into no more than half a dozen very well-defined categories, jobs on the outside don't. They come in all shapes and sizes.

Second, there is no master list. You are going to have to organize and manage your own search, collecting what is essentially a hand-picked set of contacts, selected according to your unique specifications.

Third, the real opportunities are often hidden. Although almost all academic positions are advertised or posted somewhere, many practice jobs aren't. It's almost impossible to walk into a university and through talking, create a teaching job for yourself. On the outside, however, people do it all the time. This means that, unlike in academia, you can and should call the folks who hire, and market yourself proactively.

Fourth, there are lots of different jobs out there. Whereas early job decisions in academia can set you on an all-but-irrevocable course, you'll probably use jobs on the outside to hopscotch your way across your chosen field. And of course, no job on the outside is likely to last forever.

*Your main options.* Although there are literally thousands of different jobs for practitioners, most of them fall into specific categories. Seven of these, in particular, deserve mention.

• *Free-lance consulting work.* Although exciting, independent practice is difficult to sustain for many people on a long-term basis. The work of a free-lance consultant is erratic and high-pressure, and few people can maintain the pace for more than a few years. Most practitioners eventually seek permanent jobs within an agency or organization. Some of the more successful free-lancers eventually start their own firms. Many practitioners do engage in free-lance work, however, and many who are now in organizations began their careers this way.

• *Working for a private consulting firm.* This is similar in some ways to working as a free-lancer—there is market volatility, deadline pressure, and a fair degree of uncertainty. At the same time, consulting firms are usually full of energetic, creative people, and the work they do can be exciting, varied, and very fulfilling.

• *Forming your own company.* At some stage, virtually all free-lancers dream about having their own firm. Here again, the work is hard and the market is both competitive and volatile. And in many sectors, success requires a high degree of specialization and a clear market niche.

• *Working within a private-sector corporation.* Although few corporate jobs may be labeled "anthropologist," positions as managers, analysts, researchers, and writers abound that will give you ample opportunity to use anthropology professionally. Corporate work is reasonably secure and can be very well paid, and there is usually good organizational support.

• *Working for a government agency.* Government work, although not always as well paid as the private sector, can be quite secure. The work is steady and often predictable, and good support is usually available. Government agencies are often very slow-moving and bureaucratic, however, and hiring procedures can be cumbersome. Within the government, some agencies are always going through hiring freezes, downsizing, or budget and morale problems.

• *Working for a nonprofit.* Nonprofits have proliferated in recent years, and multiple job opportunities exist, both domestically and internationally. Although salary and benefits do not usually match those of the larger agencies, each nonprofit has its own institutional culture, and many of them are much less bureaucratic and more innovative.

• *Working for a university.* This is ideal in theory, but difficult to achieve in practice. If you have a tenure-track appointment, you will simply not have the time for a career in practice. On the other hand, universities often offer a variety of nontenured jobs for practitioners—as researchers, administrators, writers, analysts, etc.—that may suit your needs.

## Technician or Manager?

Within these general categories, most jobs are either technical in nature or managerial. Although some jobs are a combination of both, one aspect usually predominates. This consideration should inform your job search.

• *Technicians* are highly skilled, highly focused individuals working in a wide range of very specific areas. Anthropologists who are hired as technicians often tend to work on aspects of data collection and analysis. Sometimes they are experts on a particular area or group of people. Sometimes they possess knowledge of obscure languages. Such people are hired because of these highly specific abilities. Although they may be full-time organization employees, they are more often likely to be engaged as short-term or part-time employees, often on a consulting basis.

• *Managers,* on the other hand, are the people who hire and supervise the technicians. Their skills are usually focused on keeping projects and programs running smoothly. They do this by planning and coordinating the inputs of teams of people, and by making sure that resources, activities, and timetables all mesh. Anthropologists tend to make good managers, particularly in multicultural situations. Although contract managers are often hired only for the duration of a specific project, they are also in high demand as full-timers inside organizations.

In your search for work, keep these basic distinctions in mind. If you portray yourself as a specialist, then your data collection and analysis skills, your command of a foreign language, and your knowledge of a particular area may all be very helpful to you. They will also obviously restrict you to jobs that require those specific skills, and this will tend, for the most part, to lead you into short-term assignments.

It is harder to market oneself initially as a manager, and here, although anthropology is still very useful, it is secondary to the broader practice skills outlined earlier. Although specialists tend to be put into the field fairly quickly—for the need is there—managers will often begin work for an agency as entry-level employees, putting in time on relatively routine tasks, learning the procedures, and writing reports or proposals. Only later will they be given independent responsibility. Although this is not a rigid pattern, it is fairly commonplace in many organizations.

One way to combine elements of both, and to gain valuable experience, is to seek work as a short-term consultant initially, and later, to move into other, longer-term managerial work. This allows you to build up experience and a track record, and to assess the various long-term job possibilities. For many people, it is both expedient and attractive to do short-term consulting at the start of one's career. With the proper skills and background, it is not terribly difficult to land short assignments, and these are often the springboard to others.

## Developing Your Career Vision

*Skills, interests, and values.*    Now it's time to focus on what you want to do and why. To begin the visioning process, ask yourself:

- What do you know how to do? What are your *skills*?
- What do you like to do? What, in other words, are your *interests*?
- How do you want to live? What are your *values*?

Answers to these questions will begin to frame important parts of your vision for your future job. Your job should be interesting, it should make use of your skills, and it should fit in with how you want to live your life (Figure 3.2).

What if you don't really know your interests and values? Aren't really sure what you're interested in? Think back over things you've done in the past, including jobs you've had, and pick out four or five that you really enjoyed. Perhaps you haven't had very many real jobs, but you've certainly had work assignments in school, projects you've done, programs you've participated in where things were required of you. And some of these were memorable in a positive way (Table 3.1).

Why did you like them? Was there a role you had that was particularly enjoyable, exciting, or satisfying? What activities were particularly interesting? If your efforts were successful, how did you determine that success? Did you feel that those jobs or activities helped you learn? Helped you achieve and express your full potential?[1]

Now look ahead: What kinds of situations can you imagine in the future that would incorporate similar attributes? What would be the "perfect" job for you five years from now? Can you describe this job in terms of sector, setting, and functions? And can you then analyze that hypothetical job situation in terms of the implied values, interests, and skills that you have used to construct it in your mind?

You'll use your personal values, your skills, and your specific interests to form your career vision. A comprehensive vision will usually include six major elements:

1. *Sector:* the general area of professional activity you are interested in.

2. *Setting:* the type of organization you hope to work with, and where.

3. *Function:* the specific things you plan to do within that broader context.

4. *Level of effort:* where do you see yourself in the hierarchy and what is your expected career path or arc?

5. *Filters:* what factors in the work situation function as door-openers to you because of your personal attributes? What doors are closed to you for these same reasons?

**Figure 3.2    Values, Interests, and Skills**

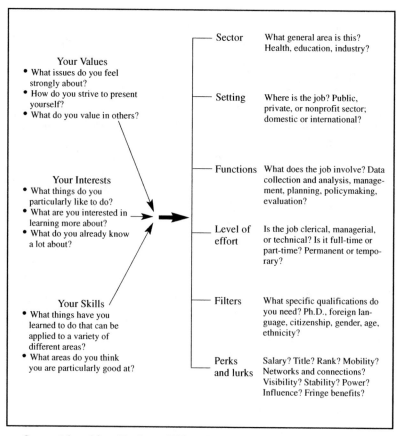

*Source:* Adapted from Newhouse 1993, p. 5–7.

6. *Perks and lurks:* this catchall phrase refers to other important benefits of the job, such as status, power, income, and the like.

As you begin to shape your vision, you'll naturally be particularly interested in how your hard-won skills are going to be used. But it will probably be better to focus first on your interests and your values, leaving skills until last.

• *Interests.* Your interests will largely determine the type of sector you choose to work in. You may be more interested in education than health, for example, or more interested in working with children than with adults.

• *Values.* Your values will help determine the setting or type of organization you work for. Your values may lead you into a life of public service in government or nonprofit agencies, for example, instead of toward a fast-track executive career in a profit-making corporation. Your values will also determine, for whatever job you desire, important aspects of what we'll term "lifestyle"—whether you live frugally or lavishly, for example; in the countryside or in the city, alone or surrounded by co-workers.

• *Skills.* Your skills will largely determine the specific functions or tasks you perform within this broader context. Are you, for example, doing survey work, office management, or project design?

### Assessing Your Skills

Once you've drafted a general vision of where you'd like to be, your skills—present and future—become easier to think about.

Go back for a moment to the competencies that were outlined in the first chapter of this book. These are sets of skills, and they are useful because they help practitioners get things done. Getting things done means, in essence:

- Identifying problems, issues, or opportunities
- Figuring out different ways to address, overcome, or solve them
- Deciding on the right course of action
- Implementing your choices successfully
- Assessing the results

- Learning how to do better next time
- Communicating these insights to others[2]

These are things that each of us will do at a basic level throughout the day, as we get up, prepare to go to school, cook a meal, or leave on vacation. At a more sophisticated level, this is also what professionals do (Table 3.2).

Graduate students, in particular, may not appreciate how many useful skills they possess. They may confuse qualifications with skills, or may assume that because they have not taken a course or written a paper on a certain topic, they have no skills in that regard.[3]

The main thing to remember is that most students possess far more in the way of skills than they think. And almost all of the skills they have are transferable across a wide range of situations.

What are your skills? Begin by looking at your main responsibil-

**Table 3.1    Analyzing Responsibilities and Tasks**

| Graduate Student Responsibilities | What Skills You Acquired as You Did These Things |
| --- | --- |
| Course work | Self-management skills. Digesting and interpreting large quantities of unfamiliar material. Presenting this material concisely in written and oral form. Dealing with challenge and criticism. Defending opinions and conclusions in a professional and graceful manner. |
| Fieldwork | Entering a new situation and crafting a positive role within it. Absorbing a large amount of new material very quickly. Applying research and problem-solving skills to specific projects and achieving positive results. Working in teams with diverse others to create outcomes that go beyond individual abilities. Dealing with ambiguity and uncertainty, coupled with pressure to perform. |
| A dissertation or project | Managerial skills, including defining a goal, setting interim objectives, developing a timetable, organizing information and resources. Writing skills. Research skills. Presenting complex material succinctly. Dealing with stress and overload. |
| Teaching | Organizing material and ordering concepts. Presentation skills and methods. Motivating learners, assessing the performance of others, and applying rewards and sanctions. Working to a tight schedule. Dealing with questions and complaints. |
| Other | Proposal writing for grants or scholarships. Presentation of material and ideas in professional conferences. Writing articles for publication. |

**Table 3.2    Relating Competencies to Skills**

| Competency | Skills You Acquired in Graduate School | |
| --- | --- | --- |
| Finding out things | Survey techniques<br>Interview techniques<br>Participant observation strategies | Data recording techniques<br>Dealing with uncertainty,<br>  ambiguity, and the unknown |
| Analyzing and learning things | Quantitative data analysis<br>Qualitative data analysis<br>Performing under time pressure<br>Linking data from diverse sources,<br>  discovering patterns and order | Making sense of complexity<br>Translating data from one cultural<br>  frame into information in<br>  another cultural frame |
| Communicating things | Communication with diverse<br>  individuals<br>Communication across diverse<br>  cultures<br>Tailoring messages and styles to<br>  different cultural requirements<br>Report writing for diverse<br>  audiences | Oral and written presentations<br>Interpersonal skills, e.g.,<br>  persuasion, tact, and knowing<br>  when to shut up<br>Negotiation skills<br>Advising skills<br>Making complex information<br>  accessible and understandable |
| Planning and designing things | Identifying problems, issues, and<br>  opportunities<br>Deciding on relevant and<br>  appropriate goals and objectives<br>Devising culturally appropriate<br>  methods and strategies for<br>  implementation | Identifying and marshalling<br>  needed resources<br>Dealing with the priorities and<br>  issues of diverse groups |
| Managing things | Managing time: yours and others'<br>Budget preparation and<br>  monitoring<br>Supervision of personnel<br>Delegation<br>Teamwork<br>Operating under pressure<br>Operating without supervision | Troubleshooting and problem<br>  solving<br>Demonstrating leadership and<br>  management<br>Collaborating<br>Coordinating<br>Motivating others to perform |
| Judging things | Learning quickly<br>Making judgments from different<br>  cultural perspectives | Synthesizing information<br>Evaluation methods |

ities or tasks as a graduate student. Then break these things down into what you need to know to perform those tasks successfully.[4]

This is just a partial list, of course, and your own list may look somewhat different. As you add items to your list, you can begin to group them into broader competencies, as we did in Chapter 2.

Don't forget to assess your self-management skills as well:

- Self-motivation
- Self-discipline
- Initiative
- Creativity
- Focus
- Meticulousness
- Stamina

- Independence
- A sense of humor
- Grace under pressure
- Focusing for a long time on a single thing
- Working under deadlines
- Thinking on your feet

## The Anthropological Advantage

Unfortunately, anthropology graduates aren't the only ones in the job market with these sorts of skills. To rise above the crowd, you'll need to identify—and be able to articulate to others—what we could call the anthropological advantage.

As an anthropology graduate, you already know how to do many things that most other graduates do not, as you begin planning your career.[5]

- You can define the shape of the world of work, identify the major groups within it and key stakeholders or influence-holders within each of these.
- You know how to locate previous research literature on diverse aspects of the world of practice, and how to evaluate the quality of that literature in terms of your own needs and interests.
- You are able to learn the "native language" of various domains of practice, and to quickly identify important subcultural differences.
- You are skilled at interviewing key informants, extracting salient pieces of data, and fitting these together with other data to form patterns.
- Finally, you are not puzzled or thwarted by complexity, ambiguity, or contradiction as you learn. You understand that meaning will gradually emerge, and you are both able and willing to revise your conceptual models as new information and meanings become apparent.

These points may seem obvious to you, but keep two things in mind. The first is that very few of the other graduates competing with you for jobs have these skills to the extent that you do. This is the good news, so to speak. The second point—the bad news—is that few of your potential employers may actually appreciate how important these skills are. So part of your task, as you develop your career plans and begin to search for work, is to be able to explain to people the nature of this anthropological advantage. Fortunately, as more and more practitioners enter the work force, these skills have become more and more evident to employers.

## Information Gathering

Now that you've made some initial decisions about your desired future job and assessed your skills, it's time to begin investigating possibilities. You'll do this in two main ways: through networking and informational interviewing.

Networking and informational interviewing are types of research—not with books, charts, and databases, but with people. Both of these information-gathering techniques will bring you into contact with other professionals who can give you information, ideas, and leads. In this way, you'll be able to test your hopes and desires against reality, and further refine your goals.

Networking and informational interviewing will teach you about people, organizations, and types of jobs in the world of practice. You'll gain insight into your aptitudes and qualifications for specific types of work, as you build a set of reciprocal relationships that will endure for years. Here again, your anthropological training will put you at a major advantage over people who've never learned to do interviews, take life histories, and ask focused questions.

### Identifying Options: Networking

*What is networking?* Networking is a systematic method of creating and managing a web of professional relationships. This is something most of us already do as a matter of course, as we meet new people, make friends, and gather information. Networking for career planning is more focused and systematic, however, providing you with information, insight, advice, and referrals centered on a particular area or set of activities.

With care, your network can be a lifelong resource, constantly appreciating in value. Initially, your network is a learning device, feeding you essential information about what's happening as you define career goals and search for jobs. Later it also becomes a reference library and support group, providing you with feedback on your ideas, comments on opportunities, and—most important—news of impending developments.

Networking for career planning and job-hunting has two specific goals:

- To meet professional people and present yourself to them as an aspiring professional, and
- To gather information about, and gain familiarity with, a particular industry.

Networking is something that you will do throughout your professional life, but you will do it during the initial phase of your job search for one particular reason above all others—to find out what employers are looking for.

Real, live people are much more informative for this purpose than brochures, job descriptions, websites, and organization charts. Although these tell you basic things about an organization, only people can provide the cultural infill that you need to make strategic judgments.

Networking is particularly important for aspiring practitioners, for several reasons:

- Any industry is difficult to break into for outsiders. Chances are, your anthropology training didn't provide much in the way of professional contacts. Networking is an excellent way of gaining entry, however, through being connected to insiders.
- Most industries actually contain a relatively small number of key people. It is possible to network across vast geographical and organizational areas with just a few connection points.
- Industries rely at least as much on peer judgments as they do on formal qualifications in making decisions about whom to hire. Who you know can be a very important factor in landing a job.
- Hiring within industries operates on word of mouth to a much larger extent than most people realize. Networking connects you to the grapevine.

- Everyone else in your chosen field has a network, too. By establishing a connection with one person, you can often get quickly connected to other parts of that person's network.
- Organizations inside an industry rely greatly on referrals, particularly for short-term jobs. Someone who was unable to offer you a job in one organization may eventually be the key to getting you hired in another.
- People in many industries (international development, for example) move in and out of different parts of the industry. As they move, your network expands and extends into new areas.

One important thing to keep in mind about a professional network is that it transmits bad news just as efficiently and thoroughly as good. You should be very careful to treat your network with respect and professionalism, and you should be ever mindful that if you fail to complete an assignment or run into problems with a job, the network will spread the word very quickly.

*What can a network do for you?* Your network will be extremely valuable to you as you begin to plan your career. Later, it will be helpful as you search for jobs. And still later, it will help you develop and improve yourself professionally.

Networking provides you with access to people and to organizations. This in turn can generate information about career fields, jobs, trends, and possibilities. Networking also gives you feedback on your ideas, your qualifications, your strengths and weaknesses, and how you present yourself to others. Your network may, as a bonus, turn up possible role models and mentors.

Networking at the career-planning stage is really a form of reality testing, helping you to answer two crucial questions: Is this a field I want to practice in; and if so, am I good enough to qualify?

The people you connect with through your network can do many things for you. They can:

- Tell you about a specific job or industry
- Put you in touch with other useful people
- Inform you about likely job openings or locations
- Advise you about how to prepare for and plan your career, and
- Tell you things you might never learn from official sources

Later in your career, networking can provide a continual flow of up-to-date information about industry trends and conditions and about possible job opportunities. It can also supply support, advice, and guidance when necessary.

*Who should be in your network?*  Build your network from the center out, beginning with friends, teachers, classmates, career counselors—in short, anyone you already know who has the remotest connection to the areas in which you want to work.

Move out to include people you have met at work, in meetings, at conferences, and at other professional gatherings. Then extend your search further to people you don't yet know. Look at websites, trade magazines, newspapers, books in your field, directories, and the publications of professional associations.

Don't neglect to network with recent anthropology graduates, particularly those in practice. You'll meet these folks at conferences, for example, or through professional associations. Ask them how they're doing, get a copy of their resume, compare it to your own, trade war stories. Above all, ask for their advice. Don't forget random contacts—people you meet on the plane or at parties. Ask everyone you contact to recommend at least one other person for you to talk to.

Each person that you talk to will add detail to the picture you're developing. Each person's responses can be used to structure and refine later questions to other people. As your questions become more focused, the answers you get will be more useful to you. In this respect, networking bears a strong similarity to fieldwork.

All of your networking contacts are potentially valuable. The most valuable of all, of course, will be people who understand the kinds of opportunities you are seeking, know something relevant, and are willing to share it with you. Each of these valuable contacts can provide you with at least one of three things:

1. They can connect you with other people. When you start out, you are looking mainly for people who know other people. At the early stages of network development, this is most important—simply generating a quantity of raw material, so to speak. You should concentrate on finding people who know others in your chosen field. Your first contacts may not know much personally about that field,

but if they know people who do, then they become valuable links or nodes in your developing web.

2. They can give you information. As you begin to develop contacts inside a field, sector, or industry, start looking for people who have specific knowledge of that field: how it works, what it does, what kinds of people are being hired. In particular, you seek their knowledge of the industry's decisionmakers.

3. They can get you a job. Finally, you will seek people with the power to either give you a job or recommend you for one.

As you build your network, make sure you document what you learn. Keep a card file or address book listing your contacts. Make files for the different organizations that interest you, and be sure to keep your notes of telephone conversations, together with brochures, information sheets, and letters.

*Preparing to network.*   Preparation for networking involves crafting a story, or script, that you will use to introduce yourself. Since the people with the most to offer you will often be the busiest, you'll need to think your story out in advance and practice it. There are essentially two parts to your story:

- Who you are covers your background and skills
- What you're looking for goes into detail about your professional aspirations and, specifically, the types of jobs, activities, positions, or opportunities you seek

You'll need to prepare several versions of this. The first is a thirty- to sixty-second version that you can deliver during an elevator ride with someone. Then there is a two- to five-minute version that you can tell someone as you both walk to lunch. There is a five- to ten-minute version that you can deliver in someone's office (which might be accompanied by several documents or diagrams). Finally, there is the full-blown twenty- to thirty-minute formal presentation, which you would make in front of a group. This latter version of your story will probably only be used for actual job interviews.

*Making contact.*   In networking, it's appropriate to use third-party referrals or even "cold calls" (i.e., picking up the phone and calling a stranger, perhaps someone whose name has appeared in a membership list), provided that you are courteous and focused when you make contact.

If you call, don't beat around the bush. The people you contact will want to know who you are, what you want, and why you called them instead of someone else. Nothing will put a busy person off more than someone who calls and in response to the question "What can I do for you?" gets a vague or general response.

It's much better to say something like this:

A mutual friend, Betty Smith, told me that you did some work with the World Bank in Pakistan several years ago. I'm thinking about applying to work with the Bank, and I wondered if you could talk with me for a few minutes about how I should proceed. I'm particularly interested in knowing whether I should go to Washington to talk directly with someone in the Bank, and if so, who that might be.

A question like this, although fairly specific, is also open-ended in the sense that it allows your contact to be more forthcoming if they want to be. And it leads, hopefully, to useful information, more names, and possibly news of a job opportunity.

It's often better, however, to write a letter. Tell them who you are, what information you need, and who referred you. Tell them how much time you need, and when you'll call to set up an appointment to talk.

*The networking conversation.* Whether you call or write, your goal is the same: to get a small piece of someone's time. If you are successful, this can occur face-to-face or on the telephone. If you are on the telephone, you will probably be restricted in terms of time, and all of the body-language signals that are so important when people talk will be missing. Your calls will rarely last more than ten or fifteen minutes, and for a busy manager, even this much time represents a big commitment.

It's important to remember, however, that you're *not* bothering people. Professionals everywhere in the world understand the value of networking, and unless you are insufferably rude, they will give you some of their time. Listen hard to what they tell you, try not to talk too much, and work to make every encounter a step forward.

Ask each person you meet for additional sources of information, and—especially—for the names of additional contacts.

A face-to-face meeting may last longer (generally, between thirty minutes and an hour), and will probably be more useful to you. Establish a conducive climate by stressing that you're not asking them for a job, but for information. Generally, people like to share their expertise, as long as they don't feel threatened or suspicious.

In addition to being prepared to briefly explain your own background and career plans, you will need to prepare a set of questions to ask your contact. If you're talking to someone who's already doing the kind of work that you hope to do someday, ask them to tell you about their work and how they got into it. Some of the questions you might ask about someone's work could include these:

- What exactly do you do in your present job?
- What do you like most and least about this kind of work?
- What are the hardest challenges in this kind of job?
- What did you have to learn to succeed here?
- What are you working on now?

You can also ask about a person's career arc. Some useful questions might include:

- How did you decide to do this kind of work?
- How did you prepare for your career?
- Why did you decide to work in this organization?
- What job strategies worked best for you?
- How did your career develop over time?
- What would you do differently today?

In effect, you're taking a kind of life history—something that anthropologists are usually very good at. Learning about someone's background will help you understand which events were pivotal in their career and why; how problems and opportunities presented themselves; and what strategies seemed to work well.

If time and circumstances permit, you can ask some questions of your contact about your own qualifications and career plans. Questions include these:

- What's the best way to look for a job in this field?
- How suitable is my background for this type of work?
- Does my career preparation make sense in terms of these requirements?
- Are my goals realistic?
- What trends should I be aware of?
- What kinds of people am I competing against, and how do my qualifications compare?
- Where should I seek to build skills or make improvements?
- What other advice do you have for me?

Networking takes time and some skill. Often, your conversations will seem fruitless and inconclusive (and sometimes they are), but eventually you will learn to ask the right questions of the right people, and then you will find yourself making rapid progress. Here again, as a trained anthropologist, you have a considerable advantage over other people in that you've been trained both to ask good questions and to listen to the answers, and fit them into a pattern.

As new information comes in, of course, you'll shift the focus of your questions, just as you would in a fieldwork setting. Ask questions intelligently; give your respondent a chance to elaborate and add detail. Ask questions that can in fact be answered: avoid too many hypothetical or complex questions. If you're not getting what you need, try asking questions in more than one way. Avoid, at all cost, questions that seem threatening or that make your respondent uncomfortable.

### Narrowing the Focus: Informational Interviewing

Once you've talked to enough people, you'll have a basic structure for understanding the nature of the work you're interested in. If networking is mainly about getting to know *people,* informational interviewing is focused primarily upon *organizations.*

You'll do this by talking to people specifically about their organization, what kinds of work it does, what qualifications are necessary to do that work, and how people get hired. Your job now is to concentrate on those organizations that offer you the best opportunities in terms of their activities, your career goals, and your qualifications.

*The goals of informational interviewing.* Up until now, you may have networked with hundreds of people, and as a result, you've gotten a pretty good idea of the organizations and agencies operating in the fields that are of interest to you. Now it's time to narrow down your list of organizations to a few—perhaps a dozen or two—and concentrate on learning as much as you can about them.

Informational interviewing is not really the same as a job interview, for the simple reason that you're not asking anyone for a job at this point. It's very important, in fact, that you make this clear to the people you talk to.

People will be much more frank and forthcoming if they know they don't have to evaluate you for employment. If you are talking to them about a specific job, they will be focusing on *you*, and doing two things as the conversation proceeds: (1) they will be evaluating you, and (2) they will be thinking of reasons not to employ you. Neither of these reactions is useful to you at this stage. Instead, you want them to focus on explaining their organization to you—its needs, its main activities, and how it operates.

In some ways it's all a polite fiction, of course. Employers know perfectly well that informational interviews are often the prelude to a job application. But you will find them much more willing to talk with you, and to share information, if you take away the pressure and anxiety that accompany a formal request for employment. The informational interview is therefore low-risk for both of you.

Although you can do informational interviewing on the telephone, it's much better to do it in person. You are interested in learning about where business takes place and what the office environment looks and feels like. You are especially interested in looking at the people who have jobs to give you, and giving them a look at you. For all of these reasons, it's best to do your interviewing face-to-face.

You should plan to do informational interviews with a fairly wide sample of organizations within your chosen field. A decent range of groups and situations will give you a clearer idea of how organizations vary, how individuals within them vary, and how working conditions vary. If most of the organizations that you have targeted for your search are in one city, you should consider making a "pilgrimage" and canvassing as many organizations as possible at one time.

Informational interviews help you understand several important things about an organization, beginning with the actual nature of the work they do. If you are doing a series of informational interviews, you will be able to compare and contrast how different organizations do their work. You will meet decisionmakers within these organizations, and you will be able, if you are well prepared, to learn from them not only about what they do, but about how they do it. You will also be able to get some idea of how these individuals see the future for their organization.

You'll rarely have more than sixty minutes for an informational interview. In that time, you should seek answers to four important concerns.

• *What does this organization do and how does it do it?* What sectors are they involved in? What kinds of activities do they engage in? How are they funded, and what is their overall approach to or philosophy of work? Who are their clients or customers?

• *What are the working conditions like here?* What are salary and benefit levels? How are these determined? What are the possibilities for promotion and advancement? What is a typical career path here?

• *What qualifications do people need to be considered for employment by this organization?* What type of personality does well here? What skills or experience are people expected to bring when they are hired? What things are they expected to learn once they come on board?

• *What are the procedures and criteria that this organization uses to hire people?* Where are jobs advertised? What application forms and documentation are necessary? Who makes hiring decisions, and how?

You should also be prepared to talk about yourself, if asked. If you are asked about your skills and experience, stress—again—that you did not come looking for a job, but be prepared with a resume, and ask, if appropriate, how your resume might be improved, and what suggestions, if any, they have for shaping your job-search strategy. Before you leave, don't forget to ask for the names of other people you might contact, either in this organization or in another.

*Preparing for the informational interview.*   Do your preparation carefully. Make sure that you have already used your network to target the people you want, and call or write in advance to set things up.

Contact people with a letter if possible. In it, tell them how you found their name, tell them you're not looking for a job, and tell them what you want from them in terms of both time and information. Finish by asking them for an appointment. Tell them you'll call their secretary to set something up (thirty minutes is about all the time you should ask for). Be persistent. Call back if necessary.

Keep in mind that it is usually not the personnel officer you want to see, but rather the person or persons who have managerial responsibility for operations. They will be the folks you might wind up working for. If the person you arranged to talk with is suddenly unavailable, don't waste the opportunity—speak with whomever they have arranged as a substitute.

As part of your preparation, learn as much as you can about the organization. This would include things such as:

- The organization's history and makeup
- Its products and services
- Divisions and subsidiaries
- Its financial and personnel structures
- Style of management
- Current issues and challenges

You may not be able to find out everything under these broad headings, but any information that you can absorb will make your questions much more intelligent-sounding, and that, in turn, will produce better responses.

Focus your questions. If you don't know enough to ask specific questions, then outline your own goals and objectives, and ask them to respond from the viewpoint of their organization and its work. In your own questioning, make sure that your queries are ones that people can and will answer. Avoid overly complex questions, multiple questions wrapped into one, or questions on clearly sensitive issues. Should you develop a real rapport with your interviewee, you may be able to probe some of the sensitive areas, but don't begin with these.

Don't talk too much about yourself; remember that you're there to learn from them. Keep in mind that you are taking up their time, and be prepared to offer something in return, even if it's just an offer to pick up the check for lunch or coffee. Often, you'll find that the people you're talking to are interested in getting information from you, and this can be an excellent opportunity to explain the advantages of anthropology in their line of work.

Take notes during your interview. Afterward, don't forget to send a polite thank-you note. The people you talk with will remember you. Some of them may even become part of your professional network. But they are already part of someone else's network, and since at some point they may talk about you, make sure they have good things to say.

*Questions you can ask during an informational interview.* You should have little difficulty thinking of questions to ask during an informational interview. But it's not an open-ended chat, and you have limited time. So you should have a loose structure for your questions, while being prepared to follow promising sidetracks if they open up.

Let's go back to the four main things you need to know, and list some of the questions you might ask for each. Some of these repeat your networking questions, of course. If you've already covered these at an earlier time with the person you're talking to, don't repeat them now, but probe for more information.

Questions about the organization and the industry that it is a part of could include:

- How is this industry structured or differentiated?
- How do the various firms, organizations, and agencies in this industry compare with one another?
- What are the pros and cons of working in this industry or sector?
- What are the future trends in this industry likely to be?
- Where within the industry is the most interesting work likely to be taking place?
- What issues does this industry face right now? In the future?
- What kinds of activities does this organization engage in?
- Who are your clients or customers?
- How are you funded?
- What is your overall approach to or philosophy of work?

Questions about the workplace itself could include:

- What are the working conditions like here?
- What do people in this organization mainly spend their time doing?

- What is a typical career path here?
- How do people get ahead in this organization?
- What are salary and benefit levels?
- How are these determined?
- What gives employees here the most satisfaction? The most difficulty?
- Can you describe a typical day/year/assignment/posting/career?
- What are the main challenges in working here? The main advantages?
- What else would be most helpful for me to know about this organization?

Questions about the qualifications of the people in the workplace could include:

- What qualifications do people need to be considered for employment by this organization?
- What skills or experience are people expected to bring when they are hired?
- What things are they expected to learn once they are hired?
- Who thrives here and who does not thrive, and why?
- What behaviors tend to be rewarded or discouraged here?
- What are the most valuable skills for people in this industry?

Finally, questions about how people enter this workplace could include:

- What are the procedures and criteria that this organization uses to hire people?
- Where are jobs advertised?
- What application forms and documentation are necessary?
- Who makes hiring decisions, and how?
- How much competition is there for jobs here?
- How would you suggest I prepare for work in this area?
- How well qualified do you think I am now?
- How do I measure up against the job candidates that you like the best?
- What else do I need to do to prepare myself for the work I want to do?

## Assessing Your Environment

Once you've completed a set of informational interviews with some organizations you're interested in, it's time to assess the situation. This involves pulling together what you've learned about these organizations, their needs and activities, and comparing that with your own capabilities.

You can do this using a simple strategic planning tool called SWOT. SWOT stands for *S*trengths, *W*eaknesses, *O*pportunities, and *T*hreats, and it will help you do two things. First, it will enable you to fine-tune your career plans, by showing you where your own background fits—or does not fit—with the employment arena. Second, knowing where you fit will then enable you to develop your professional portfolio in the best possible manner, highlighting your strong points, and positioning yourself appropriately in the marketplace.[6]

### Environmental Assessment Using SWOT

SWOT compares external opportunities and threats with your own strengths and weaknesses, and helps you make strategic choices in your job search. The external environment consists of the broad context within which work in your chosen field takes place, and the specific environment within the types of organizations you have targeted. Combined, these present you with a set of both opportunities and threats. Against these, you will set your own internal environment, composed of your strengths and your weaknesses.

As a result of your informational interviews, you are now well acquainted with the shape of the market you wish to enter, including not only the main opportunities there, but also the main obstacles. You also have a very good idea of your own capabilities and imperfections. A SWOT analysis begins by listing these in a simple matrix.

Once you've done this, the second step is to compare your strengths and weaknesses with external threats and opportunities.

Typically, you'll find that you're superbly qualified in some areas that we could call your *comparative advantage*—places where you really stand out. In other areas, however, you're going to need to do more work to develop skills or experience to match the requirements or the standards of the market. We'll call these *investment/divestment* areas. In still others, you may need to improve or brush up existing skills—to *mobilize*—in order to meet market stan-

**Table 3.3 An Initial Listing of Environmental Conditions**

|  | Strengths | Weaknesses |
|---|---|---|
| Internal Factors | What are my major internal strengths? | What are my major internal weaknesses? |
|  | Opportunities | Threats |
| External Factors | What are the major external opportunities in my field? | What are the major external threats in my field? |

**Table 3.4 How Environmental Conditions Combine**

|  |  | External Factors | |
|---|---|---|---|
|  |  | Opportunities | Threats |
| Internal Factors | Strengths | Comparative Advantage | Mobilization |
|  | Weaknesses | Investment/Divestment | Damage Control |

dards. And in a few areas, you're really unqualified—you simply don't have what it takes to get in the door. These are areas where you'll have to do *damage control.*

Let's look in a little more detail at each of these. Let's say, for example, that you have your heart set on working for a development NGO in West Africa, on a capacity-building or technical-assistance program in health. What might your SWOT analysis tell you?

• *Comparative advantage.* You may learn, for example, that because of your background in medical anthropology and your work with statistical analysis, you are superbly qualified in some respects to get the kind of job you want. In these areas, your personal strengths fit in very well with some of the opportunities you learned about in your informational interviews. These strengths constitute your comparative advantage.

• *Mobilization.* You also learn, however, that if you expect to work for an overseas NGO, you will need a better grasp of budgeting than you have right now. You've had a course in accounting, and you've done a little budget work in some of the projects you did in school, but you have also learned from your interviews that most other job applicants tend to have more experience with budgets. If you are serious about pursuing this type of overseas assignment, therefore, you will have to mobilize by brushing up your accounting and budgeting skills to an acceptable level.

• *Investment/divestment.* You also know from your interviews that although your computer skills were adequate, there are outstanding job opportunities in some NGO organizations for people who know how to produce training materials using specialized software packages for desktop publishing. You don't know these programs at the moment, although you are confident that you could learn them quickly. You therefore need to make a decision either to invest in some short training courses in these packages or to divest by eliminating those jobs or organizations that require such knowledge from further consideration.

• *Damage control.* Finally, you've learned that virtually all of the organizations you've spoken with expect their applicants to be able to speak French at a professional level. Few of them have indicated a willingness to train someone with no French. If you are truly serious about working for these organizations, you will need to do damage control by filling that hole in your resume, and quickly.

As you can see, a SWOT analysis will provide both good and bad news. If you find that you have some serious gaps in your training, you should of course remedy these as quickly as possible. But it's highly likely that, as a result of networking and informational interviewing, you've targeted areas of practice where your existing skills are well suited to the requirements of the hiring organization, and that you will be able to identify those areas in which you clearly excel.

In the example above, although you are well qualified in many important respects for NGO work in Africa, you have some decisions to make about how much additional preparation you want to do before going on the job market. Improving your skills in budgeting and desktop publishing will probably not be too difficult, particularly since you already have some background in both. Fluency in French is another matter, however. You have several choices here. One is to concentrate on finding an NGO that will agree to train you in French, by presenting yourself as an absolutely outstanding applicant in other key areas. Another is to bite the bullet and learn French, even if it delays your entry into the job market. A third option is to abandon the idea of working in a French-speaking country, and to focus instead on English-speaking Africa.

You are now ready to craft a professional portfolio highlighting your areas of strongest comparative advantage, and begin the job hunt. The next chapter shows you how to do this.

## Notes

1. See Everett (1995: 62–63) for more discussion. See also Bolles (1978, 2001) for a similar approach to identifying interests and values.

2. See Corcodilos (1999).

3. Richard Bolles (1978: 154) provides a rather nice example of the skills needed to function as a waiter or waitress.

4. See Newhouse (1993: 61–66).

5. See Louis and Atherton (1982) for an excellent early statement of this approach to job-hunting.

6. See Kearns (1992) for more detail on this procedure.

# 4

# GETTING IN:
# FINDING YOUR JOB

C hapter 4 looks in detail at the process of finding a job as a practitioner. The chapter begins by outlining how to put together a
professional portfolio. It then describes how to locate job opportunities and make contact, using your portfolio to match your skills and
interests with the stated job requirements, and writing a cover letter
that sets this out clearly. The chapter then discusses interviewing,
paying particular attention to how you present yourself and your
anthropological background to best advantage, and concludes by
offering advice about how to evaluate job offers and negotiate salary.

## Crafting Your Portfolio

You're now ready to start job hunting. You've examined your needs,
motivations, and preferences, and crafted a vision of the type of work
you'd like to be doing. Through networking and informational interviewing, you've gained considerable knowledge of those organizations that seem to offer the kinds of opportunities you're seeking.
You've contacted people inside these organizations, and talked to
them in depth about their work. You now have an excellent idea of
what these organizations do, what kinds of people they hire, and how
your skills and experience fit in.

You've also done a SWOT analysis, putting everything you've
learned together in order to determine your comparative advantage
on the job market. You're ready now to develop a professional portfolio keyed to the types of career opportunity you're seeking.

## Components of Your Professional Portfolio

The purpose of your portfolio is to create a succinct yet compelling advertisement for yourself, your capabilities, and your aspirations. Your portfolio tells a prospective employer who you are, what you've done in the past, and where you're likely to be headed in the future. The portfolio should consist of several items, including:

- A *resume* of no more than one or two pages
- A *career summary* of one or two pages
- A list of people who can provide *references* for you
- An *inventory* of publications, projects, assignments, or other accomplishments

Your portfolio is a work in progress, and it will develop over time. Employers who interview you for a job will be looking for indicators of your likely future performance. Since one of the best predictors of future performance is past performance, your portfolio should stress two things: what you have accomplished, and how you have used anthropology to do that.

Your portfolio is therefore built around accomplishments. To start preparing it, make a list of those accomplishments of which you are particularly proud. As you list them, do this:

- State what the problem, issue, or opportunity was that drove your decision to get involved.
- Jot down the relevant information, viewpoints, strategies, or approaches that you used to address the situation. Were there things about the situation that you—as an anthropologist—saw that others didn't? If so, note these.
- List the skills and abilities you used in addressing the situation. Here again, make special note of any particular anthropological skills that were essential.
- Describe the outcome. What were its positive aspects? What was this positive outcome worth to you and to others? How were the positive aspects measured or assessed?

You'll now be able to incorporate these points into different parts of your portfolio in various ways, and later, into interviews. If you can identify a core set of accomplishments and describe them in a few sentences, using the framework above, you will make a powerful impression on a prospective employer as someone who can, by using anthropology, get things done.

Let's now look at each component of your portfolio, in turn.

## Resume

A resume is *not* a *curriculum vitae* (CV)—Latin for "the course of [your] life"—which is a lengthy and very detailed account of just about everything you have ever done professionally. Academic CVs are essentially archival documents, designed to store accomplishments and present them for peer review, for example, during tenure decisions, considerations for awards, and the like.

CVs therefore tend to be exhaustive and somewhat fussy, containing far more detail than most people will ever need or want. Academic CVs can easily run to twenty or thirty pages, or even more.

A *résumé,* on the other hand (yes, the word is French, although we won't be using the accents again), is just what it says: a summary, a brief account of one's work history. Although there's no set length for a resume, most books on resume-writing will tell you to keep it to a page or two at most. It's essentially a question of how far prospective employers are going to be willing to read before they come to a conclusion about you.

An academic CV stresses teaching, research, service, awards, and formal qualifications. It is exhaustive and precise, and tends to list everything done within the above categories. Serving as a documentary record, it can be twenty to thirty pages long, or more, and it is usually not "tailored." A practitioner's resume, on the other hand, stresses skills and accomplishments, and performance outcomes. It is more general and concise, highlighting selected aspects of your background, not all of it. Designed to get an interview, it is usually only one or two pages long and is often rewritten for different audiences (Figure 4.1).

A resume really has only one purpose: to get you an interview. There are basically five parts to a typical resume: your personal data; your education; your job history; your outside activities; and any special honors, achievements, interests, or qualifications you may have. As you prepare your resume, ask yourself this simple question: What do I want someone to know and feel about me?

Resumes are either chronological or functional. A chronological resume will show your career development, listing jobs in reverse order. A functional resume, on the other hand, will show how your skills are connected.[1] One is not necessarily better than the other, and you should experiment with different presentations, and be prepared to tailor your resume for different audiences. Fortunately, with word-processing software, this is very easy to do.

*Creating your resume.*   A practitioner's resume should state the specifics of the skills you possess, highlight your experience in dealing with different groups of people and types of work situations, and provide evidence of accomplishment. Whether you are technically specialized or not, your resume should highlight your experience and capabilities, as they relate to:

- Solving problems and producing results
- Getting along with people and helping them to get along with each other
- Generating and using resources efficiently
- Finding new ways to do things

The most important thing to remember in crafting a resume is this: although the resume appears on the surface to be about you, it is really about you *in relation to someone else.* Your resume will have impact precisely to the extent that it shows that you understand the needs of the organization, and are well qualified to perform within it.

Your resume should be thoroughly professional, very attractive, and self-contained. The writing in your resume should be everything your high school English teacher emphasized: clear, concise, and concrete. Avoid fancy typefaces, and use a 10- or 12-point font. Don't be afraid to use boldface, caps, or white space, but try not to overdo the special effects.

As an intending practitioner, your resume should stress your language skills, your cross-cultural experience, the workplace skills you have, and the situations in which you have applied them. Of particular value in the practitioner resume are things such as:

- Presentation and communication skills and experiences
- A range of research skills

- Project and program management experience
- Work in teams of diverse people
- Creative leadership in diverse situations
- Problem solving under a variety of conditions

Your job history will bring these things out. Look now at the list of accomplishments that you prepared earlier, and decide which ones will be included in your resume. Don't limit yourself to academic activities—include community projects, paid work experience, and volunteer assignments. Then describe these accomplishments succinctly in the part of your resume dealing with work experience.

Here's an example of how this works. As a graduate student, you may have done some teaching. If so, this is solid professional experience. Rather than just listing it as "teaching assistant," provide details of what you did and how.

| **Skills Used as a Teaching Assistant** | **Summarizing These on a Resume** |
|---|---|
| Training/ presentation/ communication skills | "I evaluated and selected course materials, organized lesson plans and tutorials, and wrote and presented lectures to groups of 10–15 undergraduates. I organized and facilitated discussion groups for students, and advised and tutored individuals. I prepared hourly and final examinations, set essay questions, and graded all exams. I did this for two undergraduate sections of Introductory Anthropology, and one third-year section of Applied Anthropology."[2] |
| Facilitated small groups | |
| Tutored/counseled individuals | |
| Designed and wrote instructional materials | |
| Evaluated written and verbal performance | |
| Researched and selected materials | |
| Coordinated and administered small courses | |

Do this with your most impressive work accomplishments. Field experience counts as work, and should be given special emphasis. For each activity listed, itemize and specify the actions you've taken and the things you've done. Highlight what you did in terms of creating and implementing projects and programs; stress that your anthropological skills played a key role in producing results, and that you learned from what you did. Quantify things where appropriate.

To facilitate this, I'd recommend a chronological resume, and then a functional "overview" that you can tailor to a specific job. This then becomes the template for your cover letter (see p. 103).

Once you've roughed out your resume, write two or three sentences at the top summarizing your primary skills, experience, and interests. On the next page is an example of a practitioner resume.

## Other Components of Your Portfolio

*References.*  Although it's hardly ever necessary to include reference letters with an initial application, sooner or later you will make it to the shortlist, and then people will either want letters or will want to speak directly to your referees.

It is crucial to pick the right people for this important role. Although you should certainly include academic referees—including your adviser if possible—you should also try to include people within the sector or industry itself, or at the very least, people with significant ties to the industry. Your referees should be people who understand what kind of a job you are looking for, who understand how your qualifications and experience relate to those jobs, and who are willing to strongly advocate on your behalf.

You should never use anyone's name without asking them first. Many people will agree to serve as a referee for an unlimited period of time, while others will prefer to be asked each time for specific job applications.

How many referees should you have? Develop a master list of six to eight individuals who can represent you well. Make up a sheet containing all of them, and then use three or four selected individuals from your long list for each specific job application. Be sure to include complete information in your list of referees: name, title or position, mailing address, and contact numbers, including telephone, fax, and e-mail.

The reasons for choosing names from a longer list are twofold: you don't want to overburden your referees with a stream of letters and phone calls, and specific jobs often call for specific references, and you may want to ask different people to write on different aspects of your work.

**Figure 4.1    A Sample Resume**

Rachel Allworthy
1280 Middle Street
Anytown, Ohio 43760
Tel: (410) 555-6678
email: rachela@isp.com

**Specialties:** I am a trained anthropologist practitioner, with skill in a wide range of research techniques, experience in applying social knowledge to everyday problems, and an interest in working with others in private or nonprofit organizations to promote improvement in people's lives.

**EDUCATION**
B.A. (Social Sciences), Local College, 1994
M.A. (Applied Anthropology), State College, 2001
Master's Thesis: "Rapid Assessment Techniques and Their Application to Community Planning"

**WORK EXPERIENCE**
*Office Manager:* (2000–present) I am the Office Manager for Community Initiatives, Inc., a local nonprofit group in the Anytown area. The group does community outreach and planning in collaboration with citizen groups. My duties include handling correspondence, dealing with the public, facilitating community meetings, writing proposals, and preparing reports and analyses for our funders.

> Rachel provides a list of progressively responsible work experiences, and gives details of skills used and results achieved where possible.

*Survey Coordinator:* (1999–2000) I was the Survey Coordinator for Dr. John Overbeck's project on community initiatives in Middleboro, Ohio, funded by the Ford Foundation. I helped Dr. Overbeck write the initial grant, designed the survey, and supervised a team of five student volunteers who collected data. I managed the project budget of $25,000, supervised the analysis and presentation of data (see below), and helped write the final report.

> Management and supervisory skills and experience are highlighted.

*Research Assistant:* (1998–1999) While at State College, I worked as Research Assistant to Professor Howard Smith in the Anthropology Department. I collected data on the scope and content of methods courses in forty-seven different

> Research skills are highlighted.

**Figure 4.1** *continued*

anthropology departments, analyzed these data, and presented them in a series of graphs and tables. Parts of this presentation were used in a published article (see below).

*Teaching Assistant:* (1998–1999) I was also a Teaching Assistant in the Anthropology Department. I taught one under-graduate section of Introduction to Anthropology, and team-taught a course in Applied Anthropology with Professor Hiram Jones. I also helped design and teach the graduate Seminar in Professional Practice with Dr. Harry Overbeck.

*Evaluator:* (1996–1997) Department of Social Services, Winslow, Arizona. I worked as part of a team to evaluate the impact of social service programs on Native American women and children in a two-state region, under a Bureau of Indian Affairs grant. I designed evaluation instruments, trained local enumerators in their use, and tabulated the results.

Cross-cultural experiences are highlighted.

*Peace Corps Volunteer:* (1994–1996) I was a Peace Corps Volunteer in the eastern region of Burkina Faso, working in a program of environmental health education. I taught village women how to diagnose and treat guinea worm infestations, and how to teach others to avoid getting the disease. I was also responsible for producing a series of instructional materials in French that were used by other volunteers.

**OTHER EXPERIENCE**

*Study Abroad Student:* In the summer before my junior year in high school, I went to Spain for a six-week language immersion program. I stayed with a Spanish host family.

*Camp Counselor:* In high school, I was Senior Counselor every year at Hoo-Chee-Goo-Chee, a summer camp run by the Anytown Chamber of Commerce for junior high students. In my last year, I supervised five other counselors. My duties included planning activities, supervising children, leading field trips, and problem solving.

Figure 4.1 *continued*

*School-to-School Program:* In the summer after I graduated from college, I participated in a School-to-School program with a high school in the Ivory Coast. I worked with twenty other young Americans and fifteen Ivoirian college students to help build a community center for a small village. This experience convinced me to join the Peace Corps.

## HONORS AND AWARDS
State Scholarship 1998–2000
Rotary Good Citizen Award 1996

Writing skills are highlighted.

## PUBLICATIONS AND PRESENTATIONS
Smith, Howard, and Rachel Allworthy, 1998, "Who's Teaching What? A Look at Methods Courses in Anthropology Programs," *Practicing Anthropology,* 17, no. 3: 42–48.

Overbeck, Harry, and Rachel Allworthy, 1999, "Citizen Action in Middleboro: An Interim Report to the City Council" (mimeo).

"What Navajo Women Want," presentation to the 86th annual meeting, Society for Applied Anthropology, Tucson, AZ, 1999.

Language skills are presented in a professional format.

## LANGUAGES
French: FSI 3+                    Mossi (Burkina Faso): FSI 3
Navajo: Conversational           Spanish: Fair (untested)

## COMPUTER SKILLS
WordPerfect          Word
PowerPoint           Harvard Graphics
SPSS                 Excel

## RESEARCH COMPETENCIES
Survey Design & Administration       Interviewing
Ethnographic Analysis                Statistical Modeling

When you have been asked for a letter of recommendation (or when you have been informed that a prospective employer plans to call your referees), contact them immediately and give them a copy of (1) your resume; (2) the job description; and (3) a list of things they might stress. Letters of recommendation will be read to see how you stack up against the competition. Your resume says what you did. Your letters tell how well you did it.

*The career summary.*   Although not usually required by a prospective employer, a one- or two-page career summary will help you explain to others why you did the things listed on your resume. It provides a rationale for the choices you have made. It is, in a sense, an essay about who you are.

There is no standard format or list of topics to be covered in a career summary. Think instead—as you did with your resume—of what you write in relation to someone else. Ask yourself what you want someone to know about you, and what conclusions they should draw. Even if a prospective employer never sees it, sections of your career summary can be used to prepare a cover letter for a specific job.

*An inventory of your work.*   It is also useful to compile an inventory of your professional work. Prospective employers will probably never see it in its complete form, but you can mine it for material, when necessary, when they ask you for specific things you've done.

What sorts of things should go into your inventory? Writing should go in, obviously. Even if you don't have a publications record, think about the unpublished writing you've done of which you are particularly proud and which, if reviewed by employers, would impress them. Projects and project reports should go in. So should consulting assignments, proposals and grants you've written, reports, training manuals—in short, anything that shows what you've done.

If you're fresh out of graduate school, don't despair: many of the things you've done are relevant here. Class projects, term papers, conferences you've attended, presentations you've given—all of these are legitimate examples of your interests and abilities.

Jot down a list of everything you could put into your inventory file, and then begin to create your file. Store your inventory on paper, but also electronically. Consider creating a website for your inventory—or parts of it, at least. Also consider putting selected parts of your inventory on a CD. It's now possible to create CDs in the size and shape of business cards, which contain an impressive amount of text and graphics. These can be a very effective addition to a resume. Whether or not you do a CD, have extra hard copies of some of your best work available to pass out, should the occasion arise.

With your completed portfolio in hand, you're now ready to start job hunting.

## Finding Your Job

People who land good jobs share three characteristics: (1) they have the right skills and experience; (2) they have a sensible job search strategy; and (3) they are in the right place at the right time.

As we mentioned earlier, some of the most interesting jobs for anthropologist practitioners are not advertised at all. Instead, firms and agencies use their own networks to locate suitable individuals quickly for assignments that come up. If you are hooked into these networks, there is a good chance that you will eventually be contacted.

Organizations frequently need people in a hurry, for several reasons. Turnover in some groups is high, for one thing. Another factor is the way jobs and projects are developed. For example, an NGO may have bid on a government contract months ago, and only now has the contract been awarded. In the meantime, members of the team they originally proposed—containing many outside consultants—have moved on to other assignments. Now the organization must find new team members, and fast. They will rarely have the time or the inclination to advertise these jobs; instead, they will go to their databases and call members of their network, looking for qualified candidates. If you are already in their network, and if your resume is sitting in their database, you have an excellent chance of getting called.

The point here is simply this: if you are well qualified and have some experience, *and* you are there when someone wants you, you will get offers.

## Locating Job Opportunities

The Web and the Internet are good places to start your search. Some of the more useful current sites are listed in the Appendix. If for some reason the Internet has passed you by, make learning to search the Web a crash priority now.

But keep in mind what we said earlier: websites don't get people jobs; people do. Websites are useful mainly for locating possibilities and helping you research them. Your best job leads will come through other people, by way of your network, and job offers will come from people, not from the Internet. Your network will be a valuable professional resource for you, now and for the rest of your life. Care for it, make it grow, and above all, use it.

Printed sources of information about jobs abound, of course, and there's a list in the Appendix. There's also a vast range of other, more general places to find job opportunities, including these:

- Newspapers
- Career literature
- Directories
- Corporate annual reports
- Marketing materials
- Accounts of professions (books, novels, etc.)
- Professional meetings
- Internships
- Newsletters
- Company ads
- Headhunters
- Word of mouth
- Trade publications
- Professional journals
- Public documents
- Employment agencies and agency ads
- College placement offices
- Professional associations
- Job fairs

If you've done your networking and informational interviewing properly, you'll have little trouble locating job opportunities. In your discussions with people, you will have asked about how organizations recruit, where they advertise, and what criteria they use to screen applications.

Keep in mind, of course, that many if not most of the jobs you're probably most interested in may not even have the word "anthropology" in them. And also keep in mind the value of serendipity—finding one thing while looking for another. An unexpected job may suddenly appear from an unexpected direction. As Louis Pasteur reminded us, chance favors the prepared mind.

Once you've identified a suitable job possibility or an organization with which you would like to work, prepare a written application. This will consist of your resume (suitably modified, if necessary, for the specific job you're applying for) and other material as appropriate—a list of your projects or presentations, for example, an essay describing your career plans, etc. If you've prepared a comprehensive portfolio as outlined earlier, none of this should pose a problem. And if you have it all on disk, you'll be able to rework your material as necessary with a minimum of additional effort.

## Writing the Cover Letter

A cover letter will accompany your application. This, like your resume, is designed to get you an interview.

Cover letters are of several kinds. One, in response to a specific job advertisement, states your desire to be considered, briefly mentions your background and qualifications in terms of what was outlined in the ad, draws the reader's attention to enclosed material, and politely asks for follow-up. Because it is an increasingly common—although unprofessional—practice for many organizations to only reply to applications that they are interested in, you should either ask for an acknowledgment of receipt of your materials or indicate a date by which you will phone to check on things.

Another cover letter is a written "cold call" on a firm or organization with which you have had little or no contact. Your goal here is to (1) get your name and background in front of them; (2) find out about immediate job possibilities; and (3) initiate a longer-term relationship for future opportunities. A variation of this is the letter that you write "on the recommendation of a mutual friend"—i.e., at the suggestion of someone in your network who knows someone in the organization. Once in a while, the mention of someone's name will open doors with impressive speed.

A third type of letter is one to a firm where you have already had an informational interview, or where you know people. Here again, there may be no specific job in the offing, but you are announcing your interest in the organization and asking that your materials be considered. You will usually address this letter to the person with whom you have had the most contact.

Whatever its purpose, your cover letter should be brief, professional, informative, and persuasive. You have only three or four paragraphs to get your message across. You should make sure that your comparative advantage appears early in the letter, and that everything you say reflects your understanding of the employer's business and its needs, and your willingness and ability to help meet those needs.

Your cover letter will have several parts:

- A formal expression of interest in the position being advertised (or, if no position has been advertised, in being offered a position)
- An attractive and succinct summary of why you are interested in—and qualified for—the position
- A request for an interview

Although this sounds simple, it is not. Since the cover letter is the first thing that someone will read, it must represent your best and most persuasive writing. If they don't like your cover letter, they may not read any further.

Assuming they will read both your cover letter and the resume that accompanies it, the cover letter can complement and expand on your resume in several ways. First, it can emphasize particular aspects of your skills, experience, and interests that relate directly to the job in question. Second, it can serve as a career statement, pulling together the different parts of your background and relating them to your future aspirations. And finally, it can, if necessary, preemptively address any "black holes" in your background that are likely to jump out at someone who reads your resume.

To begin to prepare your cover letter, look carefully at the job description or announcement and identify what they say they need. Then match that with what you have.

Here is a simple example, using a typical job ad (Figure 4.2), and Rachel Allworthy's resume (Figure 4.1). Note that this is not a real ad (and Rachel is not a real person), but an ad put together from three actual job announcements, suitably changed to preserve anonymity.

**Figure 4.2    A Typical Job Ad**

Viva Voce Limited is a leading communications and public opinion firm. We are seeking recent graduates and experienced professionals for multiple levels of Usability Specialist positions.

> What kind of person they are looking for.

Using quantitative and qualitative field techniques, Viva Voce assists companies and nonprofit organizations in better understanding the lived experience of their constituents. We seek to provide the insight that customer-led organizations need to stay connected and responsive to the people whose interests they serve.

> What they do.

Qualified candidates should possess expertise in applying anthropological, sociological, psychological, or human factors analytical methods to identify consumer latent needs, user cognitive models, and styles of use.

> What skills you will need.

Our Usability Specialists participate on cross-functional, cross-cultural product development teams to ensure early inclusion of user needs and goals in the product development process.

> What they are expecting you to do.

Senior Usability Specialists lead the planning, development, execution, and analysis of usability research studies. They monitor trends, provide recommendations to development teams, and manage multiple project priorities and deadlines.

The pay is very competitive for private-sector work and the projects are interesting. Recent studies have included women's attitudes about the outdoors and how listeners classify and categorize music. Future projects may include work on adolescent health and sexuality, the dynamics of building design and construction decisionmaking, and family vacation choices.

The position will require self-motivation, creativity, ability to work in a team environment, and exceptional oral and written communication skills.

> What other qualities they are looking for.

We offer a dynamic, progressive team environment and a competitive compensation and benefits package.

> "Dynamic" means you are able to deal with change; "progressive" means you are able to innovate; "team" means you are able to work with others.

If we now take this ad and break it down into the kinds of skills, experience, and abilities they seem to be looking for, we can connect these needs with Rachel Allworthy's experience, more or less as follows:

| **Needed Background and Skills** | **Rachel's Experience and Skills** |
| --- | --- |
| Anthropological, sociological, psychological or human factors analytical methods | Outline M.A. courses in applied anthropology if necessary; list specific research skills. |
| Qualitative and quantitative field techniques | Research skills; survey management work; Native American social-service project; Peace Corps experience. |
| Needs identification, cognitive mapping, process analysis | Native American social-service project; Peace Corps experience. |
| Transfer of research results to planning | Survey management experience, nonprofit experience; Native American social service project. |
| Design and management of research studies | Survey management experience; Native American social-service project; Research Assistant experience. |
| Management of multiple projects | Working as a Teaching Assistant and a Research Assistant at the same time as finishing a graduate thesis and starting a major survey project. |
| Trend analysis | Project (as Research Assistant) on content of anthropology courses; Native American social-service project. |
| Recommendations to other groups | Work with nonprofit; presentation of survey results; Native American social-service project. |

| Needed Background and Skills | Rachel's Experience and Skills |
|---|---|
| Written and oral presentation ability | Publications and presentations (academic, Peace Corps, nonprofit groups, survey, etc.). |
| Ability to work in teams | Work for nonprofit; survey management; team teaching; Peace Corps volunteer work; camp counselor experience; School-to-School experience. |
| Personal skills: self-motivation, creativity | Progressive job history, Peace Corps experience, grant-writing experience. |

Several things stand out here. First, skills used or acquired in one setting can be easily transferred to another. Second, a single project or job involves multiple skills. Third, specific skills listed in the job ad are found in multiple parts of Rachel's background.

So the problem is not whether or not she meets the requirements of the job—she clearly does—it is rather how she should present her outstanding qualifications in the best light. Doing a table such as this is a good way to begin.

Setting job requirements against your background is an effective way of mapping your qualifications, and, together with your previously prepared career summary, can help you write your cover letter when you apply for the job. Figure 4.3 illustrates Rachel's cover letter for the Vive Voca job.

You will write and rewrite a cover letter many times in the course of your job search. Each job is a different job; each letter is therefore different. This does not mean that you can't use the magic of the word processor to merge files and addresses to create letters quickly. It does mean, however, that you should customize each and every letter you write to reflect—once again—the relationship between you and that individual or organization.

Writing and rewriting cover letters is also an excellent way to shape and improve the way you present yourself. Although each letter is different, all your letters tell your story, and the more practice you have in telling your story to different people, the more polished and interesting your story will become.

**Figure 4.3   A Sample Cover Letter**

Dear Colleagues:

I noted with interest your recent advertisement for Usability Specialists at Viva Voce Limited. I have enclosed a resume and some supporting material for your consideration.

As you will see, I am an anthropologist practitioner with a B.A. in Social Sciences from Local College and a master's in Applied Anthropology from State. I have considerable experience with research and analysis, and have worked in several different cross-cultural environments, both here and overseas.

I have looked carefully at your position description and also at Viva Voce's website, and I believe that I have strong qualifications in each of the areas you mention. I would particularly stress my experience and skills with respect to research design and implementation, data analysis, and the presentation of findings. I also have considerable experience with collaborative teamwork under a variety of different conditions. These and other aspects of my background are detailed in the enclosed resume.

My goal is to join a forward-looking organization that shares my interest in, and commitment to, the use of social science to improve people's lives. I want to use both my education and my work experience, in collaboration with like-minded others, to do this.

I hope that you will agree with me that my skills, abilities, and background seem to be ideally suited to your organization's needs. I would like to call your office early next week to see if it would be possible to arrange an appointment to discuss the position further.

Many thanks. I look forward to talking with you. In the meantime, all best wishes.

Sincerely,

*Rachel Allworthy*

Rachel Allworthy, M.A.

## Interviews

*Preparation.* Eventually, you will be asked to come for an interview. For academic jobs, the format for interviews is fairly straightforward. An exhaustive CV has given interviewers a very good idea of one's interest and background, and because of the relatively standardized nature of academic jobs, everyone knows what you'll be doing if you get the offer.

In comparison, practitioner interviews are much more focused on you—your personality, style, and fit with the organization. Although these are by no means absent from the academic interview, they are, in the practitioner interview, determinant.

Preparation is the key to a successful interview. You prepare in two ways:

1. By reviewing and examining your own goals, skills, experience, and key strengths
2. By collecting all the information you can about the organization and its work

Find out beforehand all you can about the organization so that you can link your skills and interests closely to their needs. Be sure to check out their website carefully and thoroughly. Research the position, research the people you'll be meeting, and research the things they've been involved in. Put yourself into their institutional context. Only in this way will you be prepared to show the interviewer why and how you can meet their needs.

Some of this information—such as the names and positions of those who will be interviewing you—can be easily obtained in advance by a phone call to the organization. Most organizations will also be happy to send you background information on themselves and on the job opening, if you ask. Some of it might also come through your network.

During the interview, you will be examined and evaluated on a number of key points. Some of this will be done directly, some indirectly. The organization will look at your educational background, your skills and abilities, and your past experience. They'll also be looking at how you present yourself, how you react to their questions, and what this reveals about your values, goals, and preferences.

Since you *know* that people will be looking at these things, you should prepare accordingly. Anticipate their questions, and rehearse your answers. The goal is not to learn your lines by heart—this would result in a stilted and artificial performance at best—but rather to achieve a smooth and confident delivery.

Let's say, for example, that you're being interviewed for a short-term consulting assignment with a government agency. The agency itself will probably give you the names of the people you'll be meeting, as well as some additional information (over and above the job ad itself) on the nature of the assignment. Armed with this background, people in your network may know something about the individuals involved. They may have done similar assignments for that agency in the past. Best of all, someone in your network may be able to give you the name of another practitioner who recently completed a similar assignment for the same group of people.

The more background you can obtain, the better prepared you will be, and the more confidently you will present yourself.

*Behavior.*   In the world of practice, there are basically only two reasons why someone hires someone else: (1) they have a problem and they think you can help with it; and (2) they like you. It's not just about your qualifications and accomplishments, in other words; it's also about personal chemistry, or "fit" with the organization.

Folks will be looking at your skills and experience, to be sure, but they will also look at your spark, your level of energy, and your judgment. They'll be watching how articulate you are, how you respond to them and their questions, and how you control or fail to control the interview. All of this is essentially related to the issue of your compatibility with the organization.

They will look at you in terms of your *personal* qualities, your *professional* qualities and attributes, and—most importantly—how both of these have been demonstrated in your *accomplishments.* They will assess these things in terms of what they see as your *potential* for their organization.

If this is a long-term job opportunity, they will be evaluating you not just in terms of their present needs, but in terms of the future. Are you trainable? Are you promotable? Can you move into upper management? Will you stay with them long enough for that to happen? All of these may be important questions that have little to do with what was printed in the job ad.

You and the interviewer are working toward the same goal—finding out whether your abilities match their needs—but you are approaching it from entirely different directions. The interviewer is trying to find reasons to reject you, while you, on the other hand, are trying to find ways to make them accept you.

Simple—but avoidable—mistakes that people make during the interview include not being well enough prepared, not listening to the questions that are asked, and not providing relevant information in a professional manner. What are some other dos and don'ts?

• *Be presentable.* Dress up for your interview. The interviewers can get away with polo shirts and jeans, but you can't. As an anthropologist, you know that outsiders are always held to different standards than insiders, so come in business dress.

• *Behave yourself.* Your interview style will be taken, rightly or wrongly, as an indication of your on-the-job style. Don't eat or drink too much, don't tell off-color jokes, don't gossip, and above all, don't run down your previous job or colleagues.

• *Be nice to people.* Everyone you meet will judge you, and you have no way of knowing, in a roomful of strangers, who's top dog, whose question is the really important one, or even whom you might wind up working for. Be courteous under pressure, tactful under fire. It will pay off.

• *Be articulate.* Talk in complete sentences that make sense. If you find yourself rambling, babbling, or getting off the point, stop talking.

• *Be responsive.* They are looking at you because they think you might be able to help them. Although your academic training is part of what you bring, they are looking for solutions, not theories. As one anthropological consultant put it:

> Companies do not buy your credentials. If they hire you, they assume you know what you are talking about. What they buy is benefits to them, solutions to their problem. One executive put this rather forcefully while berating a new recruit to the company who was taking too much time pointing out difficulties with the project. He said, "Anyone can see that the chair is broken. Keep your mouth shut until you can tell us how to fix it. Then you will be adding value to the situation."[3]

• *Be a buyer, not a seller.* You may need them, but they also need you. Maintain a positive, outgoing attitude. You are sizing them up, deciding whether you want to work for them. You can do this without appearing arrogant.

One other thing. Whatever the people want who are interviewing you, one thing they definitely do not want is surprises. Be different, be original, but don't be *too* different. As one anthropology graduate (who'd done her fieldwork with circus performers) noted after an unsuccessful interview: "The consulting company [claimed] they want people who 'think outside the box,' but they seem to want them to be inside the box while they're doing it."[4]

*Overcoming stereotypes.* During your interview, you may have to overcome prejudices and stereotypes of various kinds—some on their side, some on yours.

Academics, in the view of some outside the university, lack common sense, can't meet deadlines, don't like to take direction, and can't write clearly and to the point. Academics are often seen as impractical, concerned more with ideas than with results, and unskilled at teamwork.

Don't, therefore, portray yourself as an academic wannabe who can't find a tenure-track position—you're an anthropologist practitioner with excellent academic preparation.[5] In your conversations, project an image of someone who is both able to get results for them and committed to doing so in acceptable ways.

You may have absorbed some odd ideas of your own about nonacademic work during your time as a graduate student. Many of the folks who taught you, for example, may have routinely questioned corporate goals and methods, and may have assumed—since few of them have relevant experience to the contrary—that work in the world of practice would be boring, ethically suspect, and intellectually unchallenging.

If you, too, have come to believe that, you're in for a surprise. You'll find that job opportunities will present you with ways to learn how to do what you like to do better, with opportunities to exercise good ethical judgment and to shape corporate policy and procedure. And all of this will be much more intellectually interesting than you might imagine.

*Selling them on anthropology.* You will be competing on the job market against others who were trained differently. Although their degrees or majors may have more brand recognition than yours, keep in mind that it is what you can do, not what degree you have, that will get you a job—and help you keep it.

Your employers may not fully understand what anthropology is, or how it can benefit them. The interview is therefore an opportunity for you to educate your potential employers about your comparative advantage: the strong points that distinguish you from the crowd. In particular, it is an opportunity to explain why your anthropological background gives you a head start over other job candidates.

The strengths of your anthropology training are not primarily centered around the research methods you know how to use (although these are important). Rather, they lie in a broader way of thinking about what you do that differs significantly from graduates in other disciplines, and are at the same time highly relevant to an organization's needs.

Earlier, in Chapter 3, we mentioned some aspects of the "anthropological advantage." These centered around the ability of anthropologists to learn quickly in unfamiliar settings, uncover relevant information, and make sense of it. These are only some of the important strengths you bring to a prospective employer, however. Here are some of the others:

• Anthropologists understand that culture is the key to many of the patterns we see and to many of the problems we try to solve. Anthropologists therefore look to culture for both answers and solutions, when others may ignore this aspect of things altogether.

• Anthropologists also gain their understanding of a situation from the ground up—that is, inductively—by going out and talking to the people involved, and building up a picture of what things look like to them. This is often much more effective than imposing abstract theories, structures, or solutions on a situation.

• Anthropologists are holistic in their approaches and perspectives. They are interested in following the threads of discovery wherever they will lead. Whether or not anthropologists are "in the box," they can think—and act—outside it. This makes them very good at teasing out the unexpected and—ultimately—dealing with it in a positive and effective manner.

• Anthropologists are also comparative, and look for similarities and differences between situations they encounter. Anthropologists are very good at comparing and contrasting cases, and building up a broad understanding of pattern that is ultimately more useful than single-instance learning.

• Anthropologists are interactive. They know that formal rules and regulations are only part of the story, and that people's informal contacts generate important structures and meanings of their own. For this reason alone, anthropologists tend to make good administrators and managers.

One anthropological weakness, however, deserves mention, and this is one that many people think of as a strength. It is our preoccupation with research as the solution to every problem, the answer to every question. Research is only one way to help decisionmakers get the answers they need, and not always the best way.

Managers dealing with emergent problems resemble battlefield commanders, using an incoming stream of intelligence to tell them what they should be doing. As the information changes, they change tack accordingly. Timely, relevant information is therefore often more important than exhaustive, detailed analyses that arrive too late. Present your research skills by all means, but remember that the kind of extensive, in-depth investigation you were trained to do is probably not the only—or even the preferred—option available for problem solving, in the view of those who are interviewing you.[6]

*What they will ask you.*   Regardless of the form or structure of an interview, those who are talking to you want to know four basic things:

1. *Why are you here?* What are your motivations in seeking work in this field? What do you hope to gain from such work? Why did you come to us in particular? What was it about the job that particularly attracted you, and why?

2. *What can you do for us?* What are the skills and abilities you possess that you think would be useful to us? What in your background or experience is particularly relevant to our needs, now and in the future?

3. *What will you be like as a colleague?* If we hire you, what will it be like to work with you? Are you a pleasant, mature person? What are your expectations, professionally and socially, of us? How

are you likely to develop over time? Besides wanting a job, are there other agendas that are important to you here?

4. *What will it cost us?* What are your salary expectations likely to be (even though we might not discuss them in a first interview)? What other things do you want or need from us? Do we run any risks in hiring you? What changes in other present arrangements might we have to make if we hire you?

They may not ask these questions directly, but these are the concerns that lie underneath the questions they do ask. Other questions, too, are possible. They may ask about your future plans and ambitions (they may be wondering how long you'll stay with them). They may ask you directly about strengths, weaknesses, and what makes you special (they may be thinking about where in the organization you'd fit in best). They're looking for substantive information, of course, but they're also interested in how you handle difficult questions, whether you can think on your feet, and how articulate you are.

Anticipate likely questions. Some of these will be easy; some will put you on the spot. Rehearse what you will say. When you respond to questions, always speak positively about yourself and your accomplishments. When you make a point, use specific language and examples. Don't be negative about your past jobs or about people you've worked with.

You may also need to deal with the "black hole" problem: some part of your background that is missing, and therefore stands out. Maybe you don't have overseas experience. Maybe you don't have a management background. Maybe you don't speak Arabic as well as you should. An astute interviewer will probably spot these weaknesses, and call you on them. You need to have answers, and they need to be quick, assured, and convincing. Rehearse them beforehand, and practice them.

Concentrate on showing them how what you've done in the past relates to their present needs. Rather than simply stating that you can do what they ask, demonstrate this by outlining a problem you've addressed in the past, describing how you dealt with it (making sure to mention any special skills you used), and analyzing the outcome in terms of organizational goals.

Come prepared with five or six success stories. This should be easy if you've prepared a list of your proudest accomplishments prior to assembling your portfolio. Make sure, however, that you also include some of the "difficult" or "challenging" situations you were involved in. Present both types of stories in terms of what the situation demanded or required, what skills and knowledge you applied or contributed, and what outcomes you achieved that made a difference. You won't get as many points, so to speak, for being able to discuss a problem in depth as you will for showing folks that you had ideas—and skills—for doing something about that problem.[7] Remember, your actions and ideas are central to your story.

Try to stress two things in your overall pattern of response during the interview: that you and the job fit perfectly, and that this is going to be a great place to work. Turn everything toward what you can do for them in their situation.

As the interview proceeds, your mind will be racing as you absorb new information. You need a framework into which you can put what you're learning, and so it's helpful to remember that your concerns at this stage are basically three:

1. *What is this job really about*? What are the tasks and skills necessary to perform well? Do I have these? What other expectations do people seem to have for the successful candidate?

2. *Do I really want it*? Do my own interests really fit with what's required here? Is there room for me to grow and develop? Do I like these people enough to want to work with them?

3. *What should I do to get it*? How can I make sure they understand my skills and abilities? How can I make myself stand out to them? How can I persuade them to offer me the job? How can I ensure that I get the salary and conditions I want?[8]

*What you can ask them.*   The questions you ask are as important as the answers you give. Your overall goal for the interview, once you have convinced them that you are a charming and intelligent person, is very simple: to prove to them that you can do the job. If you know what they need done, you will then be able to explain to them, as directly as you can, how you will help do that for them. So focus your questions on understanding their organization and your role within it. Some of your questions might include these:

- How is the organization structured and managed?

- What is particularly attractive about work in this organization?

- What kinds of people does the organization attract?

- What are the main issues the organization faces right now?

- Where will this organization be in five years? What is the long-term future for this organization?

- Where in the organization chart is my job?

- What resources and facilities are available to me?

- How will my performance be evaluated?

- What's coming up that will have to be dealt with?

- What will my biggest challenge here be?

- What are my career prospects here?

- What continuing development possibilities are there, in terms of either training or new assignments?

*Follow up.*   You should do two very important things immediately following an interview: send a polite thank-you note, and verify whatever assertions have been made to you during the interview.

Although you have no necessary reason at this stage to doubt what people have told you, checking does not hurt, and it may do a great deal of good. Use your network here to help you do this.

Here is a cautionary tale, from my own experience. I was once contacted by a Washington consulting firm for a job possibility in a central African country. I came to Washington and spent a day interviewing at the firm's headquarters. The next day I accompanied the firm's president to the headquarters of a major development agency with whom the firm had the project contract.

No effort was spared by everyone I talked with to make the job sound attractive and interesting. A good salary was mentioned, as well as a benefits package. At the end of the discussion, I was highly interested, and so were they. Just before we concluded discussions, they actually offered me the job. I promised to let them know in a day or so, after I had talked with my wife.

I did talk with my wife. I also called up one of my friends, a desk officer at the State Department. "Uh-oh," he said. "I think you'd better come over here."

In his office, he showed me a collection of recent dispatches from the country in question. Reading through the past week's news, I learned several things that the gentlemen in my interview had either not known or not bothered to share with me. One was that terrorist activity in the Eastern Province (where I was to work) had led to the evacuation of many expatriates. Another was that foreign troops had been called in by the country's president to restore order in the provincial capital. And finally, the rate of inflation for the current year was just over 110 percent, and climbing.

It doesn't hurt to check.


## Evaluating Job Offers

*The structure of an offer.*  Finally, you receive a job offer. You should congratulate yourself, and then set about the task of understanding—and negotiating—the offer.

The formal terms of an offer vary greatly from one organization to another. Some firms provide a very simple memorandum of agreement, while others will draft a long contract for you to sign. All such offers, however they are written, should contain specific language about four main things:

1. The *scope of work* or *terms of reference* under which you are being hired. This spells out the nature of the job that you are expected to do.

2. The *conditions* under which the work is to be performed. These include information about your rights and responsibilities, reporting arrangements, timetables, locations, and other matters.

3. Any *special considerations* that will affect your employment or your performance under the contract. These might include the availability of project funding, security clearances, government approvals, etc.

4. The *salary and benefits* that you will receive for performing the work.

Each of these aspects of an offer can be negotiated. Negotiating your job arrangements is complex, and can be somewhat intimidating. Just remember two things: everything can be negotiated except today's date, no matter what anyone says. And everything not spelled out in writing—no matter what was said—is just so much hot air.

Most people, understandably, make money a priority, so let's deal with how you negotiate a salary that is fair and reasonable.

## Salary Negotiations

First of all, there's really no such thing as a "fair and reasonable" salary—not in objective terms, at any rate. There's only the salary that you agree to.

Some people are better at negotiation than others. Some love it, others hate it. Almost everyone is intimidated by it. Regardless of how you feel about it, you *should* negotiate. But you should only negotiate after you have an offer in writing. And when you begin the negotiation process, try to make them go first.

It's good, of course, to know something about your market worth even before you have a job interview. Interviewers have been known to break with etiquette and ask directly what salary you want. Alternatively, they may throw a number out at you and ask if that's acceptable. Don't bite. When asked, tell them you'd prefer to discuss salary if and when an offer is made.

If you have been told that you will be made an offer, start looking immediately at salary questions. Research some comparables in your field, and develop some objective criteria for determining what you will accept. Your salary should be appropriate for your qualifications, and for the job you are being asked to do. If you are working on a U.S. government contract, you will be able to obtain information on government grade levels to do some comparisons with the offer. Also check out ancillary aspects of compensation, such as benefits, equipment, working conditions, etc. Benefits, in particular, are of many different types, and some of these may be more important than salary.

If the written offer arrives before you have completed your research, stall. No one will refuse your courteous request for a delay of several days (or several weeks in some cases) to make your decision.

Once the offer is made, it will almost certainly include a salary figure. If it does, you should almost always ask for more. As long as you are respectful and courteous, you run virtually no risk of losing the offer. If the offer does not include a salary figure, you will at some point be asked for a number. Again, try to make them go first. If you are pressed for a salary figure and feel you must respond, give a range.

You can use two different approaches in your bargaining. One approach is to ask for equal consideration, with a salary and benefits package equal to people of similar rank doing comparable work. This is usually a safe route to take, provided that you can establish comparability and actually get data on what others are making.

The second approach is to claim to be special. Here, you are asking for compensation above the norm, by virtue of your outstanding skills and qualifications. Although riskier, this often succeeds in situations where organizations have specific needs.

As you negotiate, don't explain too much. Negotiations work best when neither side knows exactly what the other side will do, so don't divulge more than necessary. There is no need, in other words, to educate your potential employers at this particular time about all that is on your mind, or about what you will take or refuse. Don't make absolute statements about what is and isn't acceptable, and try to keep all the pieces in play until near the end.

At the same time, don't drag things out too long. If you keep coming back for more, or demanding additional concessions each time they give you something, you'll eventually make them wish they hadn't made you the offer at all, and this is not a great way to start your working relationship. One or two rounds of bargaining are enough.

What if you blow it? Or just don't have the initial leverage? Then try to negotiate a review of salary—based on performance, of course—within the first six months.

### Decision Time

Don't be so anxious to start working that you jump at the first offer that's made. Although it is difficult to imagine at the time you get your first offer, there *are* other possibilities out there, and they, too, will eventually come your way.

This possibility, as tempting as it might be, may not actually be the one for you. Or it might. How will you tell?

The same way you've done everything else up to this point:

through patient research and analysis. Fortunately, this time you have a set of specific questions, and an established network to help you.

It's perfectly appropriate to ask trusted members of your network for advice at a time like this. But in the end, the decision is up to you, so ask yourself some important questions, starting with these:

- *Task:* Do you understand what is expected of you? Can you learn what you need to know fairly quickly, thereby giving yourself a chance to succeed? Do you like the type of work you'll be expected to do?
- *Support:* Are there the resources to help you get the job done? Who controls these? What happens if they dry up? How crucial are resources to your own performance?
- *Context:* Do the situation and the organization look secure and stable? What are the people like? Is the job where you want it? Is the company the kind you want to work for? Are the company's mission, culture, and reputation ones you like? Do you like and trust your colleagues and supervisors? Can you get along with the key people?
- *Performance:* How are you going to be evaluated in this job? How will you be rewarded? Is there opportunity to grow in directions that you want to go in?
- *Satisfaction:* Where does fulfillment come from on this job? Will your work provide you with the challenge you seek? Are there prospects for advancement and growth?
- *Compensation:* Are you getting paid enough? Are your other benefits satisfactory? Can these be expected to improve over time?

Do you now have satisfactory answers to these questions? Do you have other, unanswered questions? Major doubts, uncertainties, or issues at this point are red flags. A red flag doesn't necessarily mean you shouldn't take the job, but it does mean that you need to find out more.

You should not hesitate to bring additional questions up with your prospective employers, even after the interview, as you weigh your options. Remember, you are buying, not selling. The decisions you make now about whom to work for and what work to do are not irrevocable, but they are important, and having to redo something later on will take time and energy.

In the end, you will take a range of factors into account in evaluating an offer: the compensation package, the place, the tasks, the organization's culture, your family considerations, the cost of living and quality of life, the possibilities for future advancement. Compare these with your original vision of the ideal job assignment, your motivations, and your long-term career goals. This is not your ultimate job, of course, but it should lead in that general direction.

Once you've made your decision, inform the organization immediately. If you've decided to accept the offer as is, tell them that, and negotiate a starting date. If you need to make some modifications to the contract, spell these out and negotiate them.

If, on the other hand, you've decided not to take the job, you need to tell them this in as tactful and professional a manner as possible. Keep in mind that what you say may find its way into the industry grapevine. It is not your purpose to criticize the organization or its work, but to simply provide a plausible reason for declining the offer. Do this with grace and tact, and you will win points.

## Notes

1. See Yate (1999: 12–15) for some examples of different kinds of resumes. See also Newhouse (1993: 70–98) and Basalla and Debelius (2001: 114–131).
2. Adapted from Newhouse (1993: 62).
3. David 1988.
4. Gordon 2000.
5. See Newhouse (1993: 53) for more on this point.
6. See Erve Chambers (1985) for more discussion on this point.
7. Basalla and Debelius 2001: 140.
8. See Bolles (2001: 207).

# 5

# Work Survival: Organizations, Management, and Ethics

How do you succeed in your first professional job? How do you judge success? This chapter will acquaint you with the basics of how workplaces operate, and will give you some essential advice and guidance about how to resolve issues, build a record of accomplishment, and develop leadership skills—all without compromising your principles.

## First-Year Survival

### Starting Your Job

For some graduates, the transition from college to the work environment can be a little bumpy. This is hardly surprising when you consider that in many ways, you're making yet another major cultural transition. And although your organization will give you time to do this, they will expect you to learn quickly.

Your anthropological training will put you at a major advantage here, since anthropologists are used to being new. Accepting that you have a lot to learn, learning how to ask the right questions, and keeping an open, nonjudgmental mind, while understanding that things are all connected, often in ways you can't yet see (but eventually will)—this is exactly what an anthropologist does in the field, and it's also what you need to be doing in your first job.

In fact, it's relatively easy to adjust to workplace culture, if you understand some of the main differences between your life as a college student and your life on the job.

*The academy and the workplace.*   One major difference between the academy and the workplace is in the degree of stability. However turbulent its internal squabbling, the academy is relatively stable, both for academics and students. Not so on the outside. Assignments for practitioners are many and varied, work environments more uncertain and changing. Some 50–80 percent of college graduates, according to one source, will leave their first jobs within three years. We have no comparable data for anthropologist practitioners specifically, but no reason to suppose that they do not fit this overall pattern of initial high mobility.[1]

Another difference concerns how professional reputation is acquired. For an academic, reputation is typically established relatively early in one's career, often based on either developing or extending a new paradigm or theory or advancing a critique of someone else's work. In contrast, the jobs that practitioners do consist essentially of working on problems and promoting changes that have an impact—sometimes considerable—on the lives of others. For practitioners, it is performance that determines success.

Knowledge is useful in both the academy and the world of practice, but useful in different ways. The university creates knowledge, by encouraging people to generate ideas, concepts, data, and theory. Within this world, knowledge per se can be a form of power. Academics are both trained and encouraged to keep inquiry going, to ramify and elaborate on lines of questioning instead of closing them off.

While it may also create knowledge, the world of practice is focused primarily on using knowledge. For practitioners, it is the ability to apply knowledge—not simply knowledge itself—that is power. However much they may love the process of intellectual discovery, practitioners usually need to make clear decisions within limited time frames, often with incomplete data and incomplete knowledge of consequences or even options.

Other salient differences between the world of a graduate student and the world of work are set out below.

| **The World of a Graduate Student** | **The World of Work** |
|---|---|
| • Focused on the absorption of knowledge and theory | • Focused on the application of knowledge |
| • Discussion of ideas | • Solutions that work |
| • Creativity and style | • Results |
| • Individual initiative and control | • Teamwork within an organization |
| • Self-defined goals | • Competition |
| • Bounded system | • Open system |
| • Tested occasionally | • Tested continually |
| • Sporadic effort | • Continuous effort |
| • Similarity of colleagues | • Diversity of colleagues |
| • Answers | • Consequences |

*Becoming effective.* As you enter your new workplace, you'll need to pay particular attention to becoming effective as quickly as possible.

You may have an advanced degree, but in your new organization, you're starting more or less at the bottom of the heap. You have no professional track record to speak of, and most of what you brought with you when you came—your degree, the school you went to, your GPA, your dissertation topic, etc.—won't count for much.

You'll have a lot to learn in your first year. Most of what you'll need to learn will fall into the category of either "functional" or "technical" skills, as outlined in Chapter 2. But to learn these things, you will draw on your existing self-management skills. The most important ones for making the transition from school to work would include being able to *interact positively* with your co-workers, *coordinating* your efforts with those of other people, being *alert and responsive* to signals from your surroundings, taking *initiative*, being effective at *communication*, and *managing disagreement*.

During this initial period, pay attention to feedback on your performance. This is what counts from now on, and people will be watching—and evaluating—your performance from your first day on the job. Seek regular sessions with your supervisor, and also get reactions from your colleagues and peers. Your questions at this stage are simple: How am I doing? What mistakes have I made? Where do I need improvement? What should I learn next?

### Specific First-Year Tasks

You'll have a year at most to settle into your new job. You will be forgiven almost any mistake at first, but eventually people will expect you to know better. To climb the learning curve, you should pay attention to three important things during this time: *connecting*, *learning*, and *performing*.

*Connecting.* Developing and maintaining relationships will help provide you with the support you need in your work. This support consists of many things, including advice, information, and (at times) advocacy. You should therefore reach out to your co-workers and begin to establish ties with them. Once ties are established, you should work to gain respect, professional credibility, and acceptance from your colleagues. If appropriate, you might also begin to carve out a little niche where your particular skills complement theirs. If you can demonstrate abilities that enhance or add value to those of others, you will be appreciated.

*Learning.* You're going to be facing problems and situations that might not have been covered in your class discussions. You'll be handed unfamiliar responsibilities, expected to work with unfamiliar and possibly difficult colleagues, and to achieve results in a busy work environment under considerable time pressure.

In many respects, this is like starting fieldwork. And as in fieldwork, if you can learn quickly, you'll survive and prosper. It helps to have some guidelines, of course, and here are four, taken from Robert Chambers, that have general utility in a wide range of situations.

1. *Optimal ignorance:* don't waste valuable time learning about things that you don't need to know about. Learn what you need to know when you need to know it.

2. *Appropriate imprecision:* when you *do* need to learn something, learn enough to make the decisions in front of you. If, later on, you need to learn more, this will become apparent to you.

3. *Sufficient solutions, not optimal ones:* don't overbuild things.

There will be other problems for you to work on after you've dealt with this one. Finish it, and move on.

4. *Opportunities, not problems:* although problems command our attention, progress comes from focusing on opportunities. Instead of looking at negatives and dealing with damage control, ask instead, "What's the opportunity here? How can we take advantage of it?"[2]

*Performing.*   You were hired to do a job. Make sure that you understand what that job is and what performance expectations people have of you. Seek clarification of any issues you don't understand, and listen to feedback.

Watch those around you who are considered to be good performers, and try to understand how they operate. Although each job is different, most successful people have a similar profile. They tend to be gregarious, social, and well networked. They are generally good at looking ahead to anticipate problems and opportunities. They get things done that advance the mission of the organization. They do these things on time, on budget, and to the required standards of quality. And they do them in ways that preserve positive relationships within and without the organization.

## Working with Others

As a student, you interacted mainly with teachers and fellow students, and you worked on your own much of the time. Relationships in the workplace are different. Practitioners work in a wide variety of situations, but almost all of them work closely with other people. This alone sets them apart from the majority of their academic colleagues, where the tradition of "lone wolf" fieldwork and research still tends to be the rule rather than the exception.

Getting along with your colleagues is now crucial to your success in the workplace. We'll look at some of the most common interactions in this section of the chapter, beginning with your boss.

### Relationship with Your Boss

Your relationship with your boss is probably the single most important factor in determining success on your first job. Although every boss is unique, there are some basic rules for being an outstanding subordinate, no matter whom you work for.

First of all, your boss is not your teacher. Teachers give to you; bosses expect you to give to them. They will function more as coaches, helping you achieve results for the organization.

Second, your boss has a style: preferred ways of communicating and dealing with subordinates, as well as specific expectations regarding your performance. Learn this style very early in your relationship. Your boss's personal workstyle may not be ideal, but it is one you will have to cope with. Keep in mind that whatever your job description may say, you are essentially there to help your boss. If your boss's way of doing things turns out to be very incompatible with your own, by all means bring this up tactfully and seek a compromise. Never forget, however, that your boss—and the organization as a whole—will expect you to do most of the changing. Understanding your boss's goals and agenda, therefore, is a crucial step toward doing the kind of job that your boss will appreciate.[3]

Third, your boss probably has a boss, too. Your boss will be involved in other workplace relationships that, although peripheral to you, nonetheless affect you. Know what your boss is up to at all times: what pressures are coming down from above, what issues are now on the table. If your boss, for example, is embroiled in office politics, or in a power struggle elsewhere in the organization, you can expect some of this to rub off on you.

Fourth, avoid surprising your boss with unpleasant news. Never embarrass your boss, with anyone. Keep your boss well informed about things, and particularly about your own activities. Be the bearer of bad news if you must, but make sure that you offer solutions to problems as well.

Fifth, do what is asked of you well, and cheerfully. You don't have to like everything you have to do, but you should do it gracefully regardless of your feelings. In your work, strive to add value at all times, and make improvements—however minor—in things by going above and beyond where possible.

Sixth, learn how to disagree with your boss. Constructive disagreement can often lead to innovation. Done well, this can make you an even more valuable employee. Most of the time, however, you should voice your differences behind closed doors. Public disagreement, when it happens, usually signals a breakdown of some kind.

Seventh, although you won't always like your boss, you can still have a highly satisfactory work relationship if you are willing to respect your boss and tolerate differences. Whatever your feelings, you need to be working with, not against, your boss. You are there to help your boss succeed, and engaging in subversive behavior will damage you in the long run.

Eighth, be willing to ask for help or advice when you need it. Some of the most unsatisfactory employees are those who don't know what they don't know. Such folks are apt to make decisions they have no business making, thereby generating major problems later on. If this happens to you, don't under any circumstances offer the excuse of "how was I to know?" That's precisely what caused the problem in the first place. As a professional, you're expected to know, and if you don't know, to recognize that and take steps to remedy your ignorance before making important decisions.

Finally, take ownership of your job. Become an expert at what you do, and always try to deliver more than the minimum required. In your work, try to be consistent, effective, and ethical. Your values—and your degree of competence—will quickly become known to people you work with. If you are consistent in your values, and consistently competent, you will become trusted. This will not only help make you "fireproof," so to speak, but it will increase your visibility, the demand for your services, and—inevitably—the quality and type of opportunities you are offered.

## Teamwork

At its simplest level, a "team" is simply a group of people who need each other in order to get their work done. Although hundreds of implementing decisions are made daily by individuals, there is always a time when teams come together to discuss and decide. Often, this is necessitated by the desire for fresh ideas. At other times, it's because no one person has the knowledge and understanding to choose the right course alone. And if support is needed from others, then very often they'll need to be involved in the initial decisions.

Although you may not have a choice about working with others, there are clear benefits to collaboration. Teamwork will help you understand that everyone knows something and no one knows everything. People think differently, and they have different personalities.

The members of a team will each bring different capabilities and expectations to the table. Teamwork will extend your own knowledge and capabilities. And most importantly, by pooling skills and knowledge, a group can often achieve results well beyond what any one member could accomplish.

Although working with a team will require tact, sensitivity, and a steep initial learning curve, there's a high payoff. Your communications skills will improve, as well as your ability to present yourself to others. Teamwork will almost certainly take you into new areas, where you'll have the support of your colleagues, and where you can assume new responsibilities. You'll get cross-training on a team as well, which will make you an even more effective professional.

Good teamwork requires openness, respect, and a positive, problem-solving approach to the work. Pay attention to how you communicate and interact. If you're having problems with a team member, don't deal with it publicly. Engage the individual privately, go over the behavior or attitudes that are causing the problem, and be prepared to listen. Make sure that your criticism and feedback are framed in terms of group norms and procedures, and that group goals are given priority.

Be constructive. Part of your job—whatever its title—is to get things done. Make your contributions to group discussions succinct, focused, and relevant. Don't just describe or analyze things; make recommendations about them. Remember that critical comment is fine as long as you offer constructive suggestions at the same time for moving things forward.

*Working with a counterpart.*  In a *counterpart* relationship, individuals are paired. One plays the role of teacher, coach, or mentor, the other the role of student, apprentice, or intern. The expectation is that the apprentice will learn from the master, and will eventually take over most if not all of the functions of the master.

Counterpart relationships are typical in technical-assistance projects where skills are to be transferred. They are common features of international development projects, collaborative projects between agencies, or projects involving multicultural teams. Whether you are a master or an apprentice, the development of a healthy counterpart relationship—often across cultural boundaries—may be essential for your job success. As in teamwork, successful counterpart relationships create synergy, and learning from your counterpart can considerably boost your own effectiveness.

Whether you are dealing with one person or several, here are some guidelines for managing teamwork.

• Do an informal inventory of skills and abilities across the team. Identify differences, complementarities, and potential trouble spots. Focus initially on the complementarities; if you are successful at developing a working relationship, the areas of conflict are likely to recede.

• Understand how team members work and learn best. Since these are both a matter of personality and of culture, it is especially important to give partners the time to learn to work together.

• Work to build rapport in as many different ways as possible. You do not need to like your team members, but you need to have respect for them.

• Keep expectations realistic and build in success. Decide together what measures will be considered marks of success, and strive for these. Keep initial efforts focused on tasks that permit the team to be successful and to share in the experience of accomplishment.

• Promote synergy. Don't seek to "win" in interactions. Try instead to combine the different strengths of individuals into a result that exceeds the capabilities of each.

• Review and revise your procedures as appropriate. Things change over time: your skills, those of your partners, your shared understanding of each other, the tasks needing to be done, and a host of other things. Make your relationship a flexible one, able to change appropriately.

• Know when to stop. Sometimes, it's time to wrap things up when the job is done. Sometimes, however, it's time to stop trying because the job *isn't* getting done.

## Managing Workplace Differences

All work environments involve issues of difference. Your workplace almost certainly includes individuals from different backgrounds, and it may have units or sections that have significantly different organizational cultures. Your organization's clients, constituents, or stakeholders will also include people of different backgrounds and outlooks. Regardless of your specific job responsibilities, you will eventually be involved in the management of workplace differences.

From time to time, difference will turn into disagreement, and disagreement into conflict. Conflict can arise for many reasons—e.g., differences in perception, values, needs, or simply communication styles. Whatever its cause, conflict within an organization can consume vast amounts of time and energy.

Like fire, conflict can be useful as well as destructive. Conflict provides organizations and individuals with opportunities to grow and develop, and the way a conflict is managed will determine whether the outcomes are positive or negative. Conflict, as Roger Fisher and William Ury remind us, is not so much a contest as an opportunity to discover people's real needs. Well-managed conflicts allow everyone the opportunity to better understand their differences and to develop mutually satisfactory responses to them. This can strengthen a relationship and give both parties all or part of what they seek within a framework, which encourages them to continue to work together.[4]

Although there are a variety of strategies for negotiation and conflict management, most center on balancing the needs that individuals have for specific outcomes with the equally important needs they may have for a continued relationship with one another. Compromise—where each party gives up part of what it wants in exchange for something else—is one time-honored approach to managing difference. Collaboration—where parties seek to identify mutual interests—is another.

Collaboration, in particular, seeks to move beyond surface statements of wants to the underlying interests or needs that drive the partners. If partners turn out to need different things, then there is often no further reason to disagree. If partners find that they need the same thing, they can often be persuaded to work together to accomplish that.

Some basic procedures in negotiation and conflict management include the following:

• Try to separate the problems under discussion from the people you are discussing them with.

- Focus on underlying needs, not just on stated wants or positions. If the issues are complex, begin with simple things. Break larger problems into smaller ones if possible.

- Use whatever common ground you find as a platform from which to continue discussions. Talk as much about what you have in common as about your differences.

- Try to learn as much as you can about how the other side sees the issues, sees you, and sees itself. Try to avoid imposing your own judgments or standards on these things. Show respect, and preserve everyone's dignity at all times.

- Look for a variety of possible good solutions before settling on one. Make sure that the solution you agree on is sustainable and is seen as acceptable according to some set of standards or measures that both sides can acknowledge.

- Individuals do not negotiate in a vacuum; each person is a member of one or more interested communities, whose interests may also have to be taken into account in crafting a workable solution.

- Avoid contaminating discussions with broad declarations of principle. When issues of principle are raised, they tend to become obstacles to resolution.

*Cross-cultural issues in negotiation.* When the parties to a negotiation come from different cultural backgrounds, the process of separating surface positions or demands from underlying needs can become complex. All parties in a negotiation are acting out their interests from within the web of meanings that their culture has given them. Cultural differences manifest themselves as differences in perception of events, differences in feelings and assessments, and differences in what people think is an acceptable response or solution. Even "facts" may be seen quite differently.

The fact that cultures are different does not necessarily mean that cross-cultural negotiations are always more difficult. Indeed, it is precisely *because* different cultures categorize and value things differently that mutually acceptable solutions are often possible. If one culture is more concerned with form, for example, while the other culture emphasizes substance and cares less about appearance, we have a situation resembling that of Jack Sprat and his wife: each party can get what it most values without damage to the other's interests.

| One Group Focuses On | The Other Group Focuses On |
| --- | --- |
| • Broad principles | • Details |
| • What is explicitly mentioned | • What is left unsaid |
| • Form | • Substance |
| • Relationships | • Outcomes |
| • Language | • Results |
| • Symbolic worth | • Practical worth |
| • Consensus | • Hierarchy |
| • Prestige | • Benefits |
| • Spirited debate | • Smooth relationships |

This is not to say that such solutions are always immediately apparent. But in a cross-cultural negotiation it is very important to avoid jumping to conclusions about what the other side needs, wants, feels, or even sees. Patient discussion and questioning, in a nonjudgmental atmosphere, will pay off.

# Management, Leadership, and Professional Development

## Managers and Leaders

The job you have today will not necessarily be the job you have a year—or five years—from now. You will eventually move into a position where you have broader responsibilities. It's important, therefore, to know something about management and leadership, and about how to build your skills in these areas.

*Management.* Managers are the people within an organization who have responsibility for setting up and maintaining its essential functions. There are three general types of managers:

• *Supervisors* are generally attached to a particular function or department within an organization. The supervisor's job is essentially to ensure production.

• *Middle managers* tend to oversee more units and more people. They have broader responsibilities, usually involving the interpretation and implementation of policy directives.

• *Executives* are "top management" and are primarily occupied with planning, strategic decisionmaking, and policy formulation. Many of them have strong leadership skills. Top managers work mainly through others, organizing and leading people who report to them.

As one goes up the managerial ladder toward leadership positions, attention shifts from the present to the future, from maintaining stability to forecasting and managing change, and from issues of time and budget to broader questions of relevance and meaning. But managers at whatever level share three key characteristics: they are responsible for *money*; they are responsible for *people*; and they are responsible for *results*.

Managers are expected to do many things over and above just getting the job done. They are almost always expected to add value in the workplace by streamlining, improving, extending, and generally "growing" the operation. They do this in several ways: by analyzing the operations to see what might be changed, and how; by hiring new people who will make a positive difference in the operation; by retraining or developing employees in ways that will improve their professional skills; and by seeking out and developing new initiatives that are consonant with the organization's mission.

*Leadership.*   Not all managers are leaders. Leaders are instrumental in making meaning for the organization and the people within it. They do this by defining goals, setting strategy, and interpreting events. Leaders are key role models within an organization: they set standards for performance, provide feedback, uphold group ethics, and reward good performance.

Good leaders share some common characteristics. To begin with, they are all, by and large, good managers. They are also highly qualified in their specialties, in terms of both the knowledge they possess and the experience they have had. They have high ethical standards that are clear to others, and a strong desire to achieve. They identify with, and have a strong commitment to, an overall vision that is compatible with that of their organization.

Although leaders are often highly ambitious and driven, good leaders are rarely self-centered. They give others most of the credit and most of the rewards. They take care of their people, even when this involves "tough love." They do what they promise, tell the truth when it comes time, and try to be generally fair within systems that are often unfair.

Because leaders focus mainly on people, they spend a great deal of time meeting the needs of subordinates, understanding their concerns and issues, coordinating their efforts, finding ways to improve group activity, and helping people succeed. They work with many different constituencies, within and without the organization, and on many different projects.

Leaders treat employees with respect, and see problems and issues as opportunities to involve and develop their people. A key leadership skill is the ability to develop and maintain relationships of trust with people. Trust, which is a highly subjective assessment by one individual vis-à-vis another, appears to be based on two things: the extent to which the leader is judged to be competent in his or her field, and the extent to which the leader's values appear clear and consistent.

*You'll learn that . . .*   As you move up the managerial ladder, you will come to understand a few basic realities. For one thing, there are rarely right or wrong answers to the problems managers must deal with: only consequences that follow their decisions and form the basis for subsequent decisions. Problems tend to be open-ended, and seemingly never-ending.

People who move into management sense an immediate change in their relationships with other people. With subordinates, it's no longer really possible to be a "buddy," and people will start looking to you for advice and answers rather than friendship.

With other managers, you'll now find that although you don't have nearly as much authority as you once thought managers had, you do have vastly increased responsibility for results within your area. You've probably inherited a number of thorny problems and unfamiliar responsibilities, and in some areas the stakes will be higher than you might have imagined. The learning curve for a new manager is often quite steep, and seems to keep going up for a very long time.

## Delegation

Since managers and leaders work largely through others, delegation becomes the principal way in which their work gets done. If—like many anthropologists—you've been used to working on your own, you may have some trouble at first with the idea of delegating work to others. Delegation is an art, involving decisions about what to delegate, whom to delegate to, how to ensure success, and what to do in case of problems.

Deciding what to delegate, and to whom, is your first task. Begin with an inventory of your current jobs, tasks, projects, and responsibilities. Write them down, and arrange them in an order that makes sense to you. Now divide them into things that you want or need to control yourself, and things that could be done by others.

As a general rule of thumb—and assuming you have the personnel to handle it—anything that *can* be done by someone else *should* be done by them. You can delegate by task, by goal, or by function. Delegate important as well as routine jobs. It's not just about relieving yourself of unnecessary work; it's primarily about bringing your team together as a working unit, and building capacity in each individual member.

Now look at your team. Each person has different skills and abilities. Each is better at some things than others. Of the different tasks and responsibilities that you have decided to delegate, who on your team has an interest in specific ones? Who has the ability to do them well? Who has the time? Pick people who you are fairly confident can handle the assignments you give them. Again, as a rule of thumb, choose the most junior person who's capable. In that way, you will build up the capacities of your team.

Suppose no one on your team has the ability to carry out a delegated assignment. Should you invest time and money in training your staff members so that they can do the job, or should you hire an outside consultant to do it for you? If it's something you'll need to have done on a regular basis, you will probably choose to invest in training. For onetime jobs, however, it might be better to hire a consultant.

Once you have decided what to delegate, and to whom, call in your team members and explain what you need from them. The coordination of delegated tasks is very important, to get things done as efficiently as possible, while keeping people from duplicating efforts and getting in each other's way.

Define the project or assignment clearly. Explain its purpose and importance, the deadline for completion, and any special considerations that apply (e.g., budget limits, procedures, etc.). Deadlines are particularly important.

If necessary, write the assignments out. Make sure that people understand what responsibilities they have and what they are expected to deliver. Explain what authority over resources they will be given. Give everyone a chance to ask questions and clarify expectations.

Once your teams start working on their assignments, be sure to provide them with the support they need, while at the same time allowing them the flexibility and autonomy to carry out tasks as they see fit. Remain accessible to them, but don't micromanage, and don't solve their problems for them unless there is a clear risk of failure or damage.

Delegation doesn't mean that you lose control of what's happening, but it does mean giving the job to someone else and letting them do it their way. By definition, it won't be exactly the way you'd have done it yourself. But if you have confidence in your team, and if you've made the overall requirements clear, you can step out of the way and let people get on with the job. When tasks have been completed, provide your team members with praise and recognition for their efforts.[5]

## Fixing Performance Problems

As the amount of work that you delegate increases, you're almost certain to encounter performance problems from time to time. Knowing how to diagnose and resolve performance problems is therefore a key managerial skill. There are three steps to this: identifying the problem, diagnosing the problem, and responding to it (Figure 5.1).

Identifying the problem can be done by carrying out an analysis of the difference between desired performance and what you are getting now. Don't jump to premature conclusions; wait until you understand the situation. Review the requirements for performance and how these have been expressed to the employee(s) in question. Collect as much information as you can about the deficient performance; since most tasks are complex ones, it is very helpful at this stage if you can attempt to pinpoint exactly where performance falls short.

Early in this process, you will want to ask an important question: Although performance isn't up to standard, do I care? If you don't really care (e.g., if the underperformance is trivial, or if it only occurs once in a blue moon, or if the costs of fixing it are out of all proportion to its importance), then you may want to quietly back away.

Otherwise, you will need to take the next step, which is that of diagnosis: finding out why the gap in performance is occurring.

Performance problems that are centered on employees tend to be of two basic types: those that are due to a lack of skills, and those due to other things. If employees do not have the requisite skills, or if they once had them but no longer, you have a variety of options for resolution, ranging from training and feedback through extra practice and—at an extreme—taking the employee off the job.

**Figure 5.1   Resolving Performance Problems**

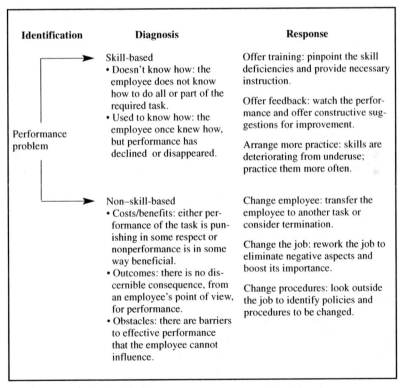

| Identification | Diagnosis | Response |
|---|---|---|
| | Skill-based | Offer training: pinpoint the skill deficiencies and provide necessary instruction. |
| | • Doesn't know how: the employee does not know how to do all or part of the required task. | |
| Performance problem | • Used to know how: the employee once knew how, but performance has declined or disappeared. | Offer feedback: watch the performance and offer constructive suggestions for improvement. |
| | | Arrange more practice: skills are deteriorating from underuse; practice them more often. |
| | Non–skill-based | Change employee: transfer the employee to another task or consider termination. |
| | • Costs/benefits: either performance of the task is punishing in some respect or nonperformance is in some way beneficial. | |
| | • Outcomes: there is no discernible consequence, from an employee's point of view, for performance. | Change the job: rework the job to eliminate negative aspects and boost its importance. |
| | • Obstacles: there are barriers to effective performance that the employee cannot influence. | Change procedures: look outside the job to identify policies and procedures to be changed. |

*Source:* Adapted from Mager and Pipe 1970, p. 3.

If the problem is not due to a lack of skills, then other, more complex, factors may be involved. Employees may be experiencing negative consequences for task performance (or, alternatively, positive consequences for nonperformance). These may be located outside the immediate work context itself, and therefore are difficult to identify. Nonperformance may also be due to a perception—accurate or not—that performance has no real consequences one way or the other. And finally, there may be procedural obstacles that interfere with performance. Again, these may lie well outside the immediate context.

Here again, a series of options is available, ranging from employee transfer or termination to making changes in the nature of the job itself (including setting up appropriate incentives and/or sanctions), or, going further afield, changing the policies, rules, and conditions under which the job is performed.

Once you've gone through these steps, you should set up a performance plan to monitor performance from now on. If problems still remain, you will have to decide whether you can in fact effect change in these, or whether the better course of action is to modify your own plans and expectations.[6]

## Professional Development

Whether you are interested in staying in your present job or moving to another one eventually, it's useful to think about professional development: getting better at what you do, getting recognition for your accomplishments, learning new things, and exploring new areas.

Whether you stay in one job or move through several, you'll need to pay attention to developing yourself, if for no other reason than to keep abreast of changes in your work environment. Developments in technology, increases in knowledge, shifts in your client populations—these and other changes make retraining necessary.

But you can also develop yourself professionally to advance—to move into progressively responsible positions, to gain influence and authority, to increase your leadership abilities, and to achieve more professional satisfaction. And as you advance yourself, you are also advancing your discipline. For all these reasons, you'll want to be as good as you can be.

You are surrounded by opportunities to develop as a professional. Every job you do, every contact you make, and every assignment you take can add something to your capabilities. Sometimes, you will gain information about how something works, about how people in a particular part of the world live, or about how a problem is put together. At other times, you learn technique—how to do something under a particular set of circumstances. And at other times, you learn about what to do next—where future opportunities lie.

Several key strategies for doing these things are outlined below.

*Understanding your organization thoroughly.* Begin by becoming an expert on your own organization. Determine where the influence lies, how decisions are made, and what the key issues are. Identify leaders and learn about what they do and how they operate. Develop relationships with them if at all possible. If you aspire to become like them someday, start modeling aspects of your behavior on what they do. Even if you have no interest in stepping into a leader's shoes, understanding how he or she operates will help you do your own work.

*Seeking visibility.* It's usually harder to achieve visibility from the lower ranks in an organization. It gets easier, for the most part, as you move up. In any case, you should do two basic things from the outset: join in, and show people what you can do. This can be accomplished in many different ways: through membership in clubs and associations, through workshops and speeches, or through publishing. Keep in mind that negative publicity can just as easily come your way, if you are not careful.

Visibility will bring you opportunities, and can be enhanced in several ways. Try to get assigned to projects that are themselves highly visible. Develop a specialty that will bring you into the spotlight from time to time. Seek the kinds of jobs that bring you into contact with a highly diverse group of people, in and out of the organization.

Seek promotion as a way to become more visible. Become thoroughly familiar with how performance assessment is done within your organization, and how such assessments are linked (or not linked) to promotions and raises. Every organization will have some sort of review process, even if it is highly subjective and haphazard.

Knowing how this is done will help you understand what you need to do to move up.

*Maintaining your network.*   Keep expanding your professional network. You will come into constant contact with other professionals whose experience, knowledge, and insights can complement your own. Each new contact is an opportunity to learn new and interesting things. One practitioner emphasizes:

> Not only is participation in professional networks important to our development as practicing anthropologists, it is also crucial for the advancement of our discipline. Participation in professional networks is a process through which we derive our identity, through which we stay current with the discipline, and through which we are able to contribute to the discipline. Perhaps it is time for us to collectively and proactively acknowledge the value of the professional network as something that holds us together, our common thread.[7]

Don't restrict your networking to folks like yourself; develop relationships with other specialists who have different backgrounds, and see what their perspectives can teach you about your own.

You can network in many different ways. Presenting your work to outside groups is an excellent way to meet new people and learn from them. If you're community-minded, work on interesting projects with others. Offer to teach or mentor someone else. Join an association of specialists in a field connected to your own. In these and other ways, you'll gain professionally.

*Seeking significant challenges.*   Get involved in things that matter to the organization. Use the experience you gain from doing these things to do other things of importance. If you have paid attention to upper management, you will understand what their needs and priorities are. Choose opportunities within this overall frame.

If, on the other hand, you work for the type of organization that does *not* have clearly articulated priorities, or which is floundering, you can still contribute. Determine what the key issues are facing the people in your reference group, what skills people need to deal with these issues, and what strategies seem to be effective. Learn how to do these things if possible. Volunteer for assignments that will give you this kind of experience.

*Taking on new assignments.*  New assignments open new doors, and are always prime occasions for new learning. Taking on a new assignment may open up career options down the road. In my own case, for example, learning how to collect data for development projects led to assignments where I was asked to design projects. This experience led in turn to opportunities to manage projects, and then programs. And this in turn led me into policy work.

Almost all organizations have certain rites of passage that are obligatory for anyone seeking to rise. So even though a particular assignment might not be your first choice, it may be the wise choice, if you are eventually headed somewhere beyond where you are now.

Often, you don't have much control over new assignments: they are given to you, either by a boss or a client, or they materialize from the headlines, and you have to respond. But in other cases, you can choose what you do next. Here, you should try to extend yourself as much as you can, while building on past accomplishments.

Seek new assignments in different areas that you're curious about. Look for ones that are unusual, that are broadly focused rather than narrow, and that require you to consult and interact with people outside your own area of specialization. In this way, you will be forced to explore new areas.

Choose assignments that are longer rather than shorter, and that require you to do some actual research and document it in a report or presentation. Short assignments (particularly those that have very tight deadlines) predispose professionals to seek approaches and answers from the stock of what they already know, rather than allowing them to explore and develop new avenues. Being required to present your findings will help reinforce your learning.

*Learning outside the job.*  New assignments aren't the only way to learn, of course. You can also learn from—and through—your network by creating an "advisory board": a group of senior professionals who are willing to advise you from time to time about job issues and career choices. Use your advisory board not only for insight and information, but also, from time to time, for feedback on your performance.

Sometimes, what you need to learn can't be gotten on the job. In that case, you should consider arranging for outside training. Look for evening or weekend courses to take, for example. Attend lectures, workshops, and other programs in areas that interest you. Map out a reading program.

*Doing it mainly by yourself.*   Maintaining professional competence as an anthropologist practitioner is largely up to you as an individual. If you are lucky enough to work for an organization that understands the value of professional development, then many of your opportunities to learn and extend yourself can come through them. If not, you will need to seek out resources and opportunities on your own.

You may get little help from the anthropological establishment. Yearly conferences apart, the discipline itself has virtually no system for retraining practitioners, and has shown little interest so far in doing this. This is a situation that will not continue indefinitely, and eventually practitioners will take charge of their own retraining. For the moment, however, if you want to maintain yourself professionally, you will need to find ways to do it yourself.

## Working with a Mentor

Earlier, we discussed how important academic advisers can be to you in shaping your career. Now let's look at mentors in terms of their impact on your professional development.

A mentor is a person who helps to oversee and guide the career development of another person. Mentors teach; mentors provide counseling, coaching, and support; mentors intervene; and mentors advocate or sponsor. Mentors provide their charges with role models, feedback, criticism, and challenges.[8]

*One mentor or several?*   Many organizations have formal mentoring programs. Mentoring programs can help organizations in orienting new hires and spotting talent—grooming understudies, as it were, for key management positions.

Whether or not your organization has a program, you should probably seek one or more mentors outside your organization as well. Your job has different aspects or facets to it, and often, one mentor can't cover all the bases. Not every professional sees problems the same way; not everyone solves problems in similar fashion. Having more than one mentor will broaden your understanding of both the range of situations professionals work in and the variety of strategies and approaches they use in these situations.

If, for example, you're working in international development for an NGO, you may have a mentor within your own organization. You might have another mentor, however, within a bilateral or multilateral agency, another within a university institute, and still another within a consulting firm that works overseas. Each of these individuals can provide you with different personal and professional perspectives.

*Choosing a workplace mentor.* At least one of your mentors, however, should be within your present organization. You do not need to hitch yourself to a rising star (although that might be a good idea in some cases), but you should have someone at work who cares about seeing your career advance, and who is senior enough to provide both insight and a push in the right direction from time to time.

It's often not that easy to attract a suitable mentor. It's not just a question of your choosing someone—they also have to choose you. The best way to develop a good mentoring relationship is to take your time, look at a variety of people within your network, and while you are doing this, keep yourself as visible as you can in a variety of different organizational settings. People will not usually accept you as a mentee until they have watched you perform for a while. Give them a chance to do that.

Just as you did with your adviser, choose your mentor(s) carefully. Once you've identified someone who might make a good mentor, it is perfectly appropriate to take the initiative. Often, the best entry point is offering to help your potential mentor with something they're working on.

Ideally, you want someone who is good at what they do, is secure and well-considered within the organization, and who has been around long enough to know how things really work. You should also look for someone who is a good teacher and motivator, but who is also able to tell you unpleasant truths on occasion. Stay away from outsiders or marginal individuals, even if they are very creative; if they are not part of the inner circle, they will not be as helpful to you in understanding how decisions get made.

The person you choose should be able to help you, but more importantly, he or she should *want* to help you, and should understand how to do that. Often, potential mentors are simply too busy, or too pressured, to have the time and energy to devote to you. And, of course, your mentor should be someone whom you personally like and feel comfortable working with.

*What a mentor can give you.*   If you are lucky enough to have a mentor inside your own organization, you can learn a great deal from him or her. Your workplace mentor can provide you with insight that normally comes only after years of experience.

For example, your mentor can tell you about the power structure of the organization, how to deal with it, and whom and what to avoid. Your mentor can introduce you to the right people, recommend the courses of action that will be most likely to move you ahead in the organization, and warn you when you're about to do something stupid.

Your mentor can show you shortcuts, and provide honest feedback on your performance. Your mentor can also help you envision the future by pointing out the likely situations and choices that you will face later on, and how to best deal with these.

The best mentors can be inspirational role models. Observing your mentor closely over time will teach you a lot about how success is defined and demonstrated within your organization.

*The mentoring relationship.*   Whether inside or outside your organization, mentoring should be a two-way exchange. No matter how much you gain from your mentor, be prepared to give something back. Don't expect miracles from your mentor, and don't assume that the relationship will always be a positive one. Finally, don't expect that each of your mentoring relationships will be similar.

Mentoring relationships don't usually remain stable. Although a mentoring relationship may last a lifetime, there will be an initial period during which the relationship is initiated, followed by a longer time during which the relationship is defined. Eventually, the relationship will change, often to one that is less intense.

This can happen for many reasons. You or your mentor may have changed jobs, for example, or one of you has moved into new areas of interest or responsibility. Perhaps you have both simply exhausted the exchange possibilities in the relationship, and it is now time to move on. At this point, you and your mentor may drift apart, or you may continue your relationship in a redefined way.

Mentoring is not without its perils, of course. Mentors and their protégés may have conflicts of interest—open or hidden—that get in the way of an effective relationship. They may have hidden agendas. Either of these can be damaging, if not hazardous, to one or both of the individuals involved.

Although your mentor can protect you to some extent within the organization, if your mentor falls from grace, so will you. Alternatively, your mentor may let you down or fail to protect you. In the worst case, your mentor may betray you in some way. Although these are unlikely scenarios, they are possible, and you should keep them in mind.

The boundaries of the mentoring relationship are also sensitive. When does the provision of support and advice turn into running someone's life? When does professional admiration turn into romantic attachment? When does a sincere interest in you as an aspiring professional become intrusive manipulation? Again, attention to the structuring of the mentoring relationship, combined with a willingness to review and revise the arrangements from time to time, will prevent problems.

## Professional Writing

### The Importance of Writing

Successful professionals are good communicators. They communicate in many different ways—through presentations, meetings, face-to-face encounters, etc. But one very important way they communicate is through writing.

As a form of communication, writing has some special advantages. Because it's not real-time communication, writers can take time with drafting, revising, and reworking, searching for just the right word or phrase. Because they control style, vocabulary, and format, they can deliberately temper their emotions, if necessary, while they consciously set out to excite others. Good writing can be very persuasive.

Writing is a permanent record, and acquires a certain legitimacy simply because it's written down. You can reach large numbers of people through the written word, over long distances and periods of time. We're still reading Shakespeare, for example, as well as *Beowulf,* the Bible, and . . . well, you get the idea.

### The Difficulty of Writing Well

Unfortunately, not all of us are good writers. Academically trained people, in particular, seem not to be. One writer, a former professor turned journalist, decries what he terms the "footnote mentality" of much academic writing. He defined this as follows:

> The obsession for detail coupled with a penchant for exploring every distracting land and byway that opens off the main road of the argument . . . seems to characterize much of today's scholarship. Such thinking turns inward upon itself, all but shutting out even the most literate non-specialist. It produces writing that is sometimes praised but rarely read—aloof, self-satisfied, jargon-rich, and convoluted. This mentality works a bit like Boston street signs, which I've always believed are designed to remind you that if you haven't figured out how to get to your destination, you don't deserve to know.[9]

The sociologist Howard Becker notes that students are trained to believe that the more difficult the writing style, the more intellectual one is supposed to be. He quotes one of his students as follows: "When I read something and I don't know immediately what it means, I always give the author the benefit of the doubt. I assume this is a smart person and the problem with my not understanding the ideas is that I'm not as smart."[10] If graduate students learn to think this way—and we can probably agree with Becker that many of them do—then it is not surprising that later on they will reflect this thinking in their own writing.

We also know, of course, that our colleagues in anthropology departments are no different from others in this respect. Sandy Ervin offers this observation: "The most serious problem [with anthropology] is that much of the anthropological literature is neither accessible nor useful to the public or policy makers. Anthropologists' writings have been either filled with details or overburdened with theory and jargon. There may be few direct recommendations or even explicit recognition or understandings of the problems that need to be solved."[11]

Clarity, precision, and directness, although certainly culturally embedded in our own society, are probably useful the world over if you want to get your point across, much more so than the essentially ceremonial style of academic writing that seems to have found its way into most of the world's universities. As a practitioner, you will need to be able to analyze, order, and present information, and do it persuasively, simply, and quickly.

## Effective Writing

All successful writing speaks directly to the needs of the audience. Knowing your audience will help you make important decisions about the content of your communication, its overall purpose, and how it should be presented. Whenever you communicate important ideas, you should be clear in your own mind about who you are speaking to, what you want them to remember, and what you want them to do afterward.

You'll need to plan what you want to say carefully. Elizabeth Cohn and Susan Kleimann suggest looking at four elements in the writing process, and connecting them.

These four elements do not structure the writing itself, but help to structure the *thinking* that leads up to the point when pen meets paper. If you understand whom you are writing for and what they need, you will be able to decide what information is most relevant, what the significance of that information is, and how to present your case most effectively.

In the process, you will shift from thinking of the writing as "yours" and begin thinking of it as "theirs"—as belonging to your audience, to be used by them for their own specific purposes.

**Figure 5.2   Elements of the Writing Process**

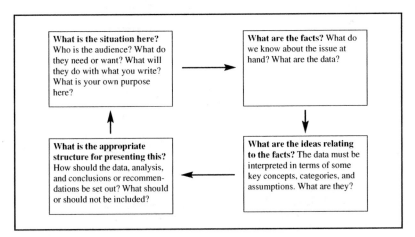

*Source:* Adapted from Cohn and Kleimann 1989, p. 4.

*Writing as rewriting.*   The key to good writing, as any professional will tell you, is rewriting. You simply cannot start a major piece of writing the night before (as you may have learned to do as an undergraduate) and expect to dash it off in one draft. Generally, experienced writers go through several—often many—drafts before they are satisfied. So although the four elements presented above are not a structure for the essay itself, they will continue to guide your thinking as you proceed with the drafting or rewriting necessary to translate your thoughts to paper.

The classic essay structure, which you probably learned in school, is highly adaptable, and will serve you well as a template for much of what you write. It is clean, clear, and simple, and will help you present your thoughts in an effective way.

In the *introduction,* you will want to review (for yourself, if not explicitly) what your purpose in writing is: what you want your readers to know, feel, and eventually do. You will need to have a strong and clear statement of your thesis or theme. You are not writing a mystery story, so get your intentions out in front of the reader as soon as possible.

In the *body* of what you write, state your main points clearly and

**Figure 5.3   A Three-Part Structure for Persuasive Writing**

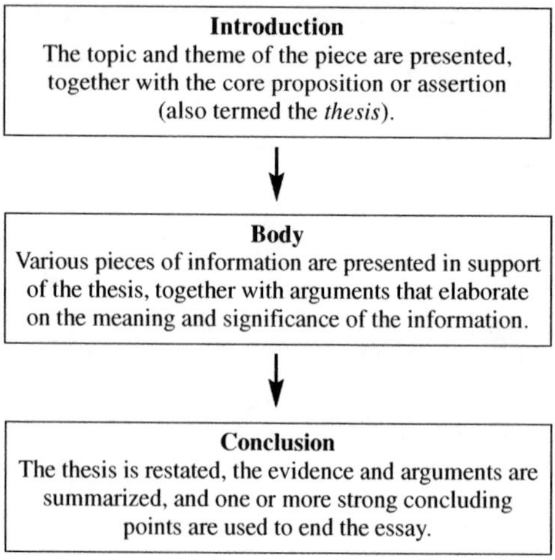

**Introduction**
The topic and theme of the piece are presented, together with the core proposition or assertion (also termed the *thesis*).

↓

**Body**
Various pieces of information are presented in support of the thesis, together with arguments that elaborate on the meaning and significance of the information.

↓

**Conclusion**
The thesis is restated, the evidence and arguments are summarized, and one or more strong concluding points are used to end the essay.

*Source:* Adapted from Howard and Barton 1986.

concisely, and structure their presentation for maximum effect. Buttress your evidence with elaboration (providing more details), illustration (providing examples), and argumentation (providing reasons).

Put your best points first, while preempting any objections that you know will surface in readers' minds. Connect your points with appropriate transitions, and move smoothly and quickly through them. If necessary, reinforce the significance of what you are saying in terms that readers can understand, such as economic costs and benefits. Use graphics and special formatting (e.g., bold, italics, capitals, white space, etc.) to help make your points.

In the *conclusion,* go back again to the theme or thesis and restate it, reviewing quickly the ground you've covered and pulling everything together neatly. If you can, end on a snappy, thought-provoking note.

Improving your writing abilities is a lifelong process. Read widely, look for good role models, and learn from what they do. You will eventually develop your own distinctive style, or writing voice, as you gain experience with professional writing.

## Ethics for Practitioners

### The Development of Anthropological Ethics

Ethics—the rules or standards governing personal and professional conduct toward others—is a crucial aspect of practice, and has been extensively debated within anthropology.

The first ethics statement in American anthropology came from the Society for Applied Anthropology in 1948 (revised in 1983). The American Anthropological Association issued a statement on ethics in 1967, followed by the "Principles of Professional Responsibility" in 1971 (revised in 1997). The National Association for the Practice of Anthropology produced its "Ethical Guidelines for Practitioners" in 1988.[12]

The AAA's 1997 code of ethics stresses three points in particular: don't do harm to anyone if you can possibly help it; don't deceive people or misrepresent either yourself or what you are doing; and try to be as impartial as possible. As statements, these are sensible and uncontroversial. In practice, of course, they are very difficult to both interpret and apply.

A pivotal point in the development of anthropological ethics—
and one that underlies ethics talk even today—was the experience of
the Vietnam War, which triggered a firestorm of controversy within
anthropology. One result was a suspicion of applied work that lingers
until this day.

*Themes in anthropological ethics.*    Several key themes inform
discussions of anthropological ethics. One of them—arising directly
out of the Vietnam experience—involves secrecy, clandestine
research, and confidentiality. Another centers on the morality of the
powerful doing research upon the powerless.

Perhaps one of the most important and enduring aspects of the
ethics discussion is that relating to telling the truth—i.e., to the public dissemination of what anthropologists have learned and what they
think it means. Many within the discipline feel that anthropologists
have not only an obligation to seek and know the truth, but to *tell* the
truth, openly and publicly. As Gerald Berreman says, "If we do not
fulfill this responsibility, we are nothing more than human engineers—hirelings in the service of any agency with any agenda that
can buy our expertise."[13]

*Issues and problems with ethics.*    There are some significant problems with the way ethics in anthropology has developed. Although
the anthropological literature on ethics is extensive, it is almost
exclusively centered on academic concerns. The cases presented tend
to focus primarily on field research situations, and only secondarily
on relationships with students, other colleagues, or funding agencies.
We have very few published accounts of the ethical dilemmas faced
by practitioners.

There is also little discussion of the ethical concerns of other
stakeholders, including other professionals, and of how these might
coincide with—or differ from—those of anthropologists. Anthropologists talking about ethics are talking mainly to one another; there
is little acknowledgment of the fact that in a culturally diverse world,
there are bound to be diverse ethical perspectives, and that sooner or
later an anthropologist will encounter these.

Furthermore, there is no real agreement within the discipline as
to what might constitute anthropological "malpractice," and what, if
anything, might be done about it. None of our codes have what might
be termed sharp teeth, and the discipline has few established proce-

dures for dealing with transgression. It is perhaps significant that in the history of the AAA, only one anthropologist has ever been officially censured, and that was Franz Boas, early in the last century. Attempts to devise systems of certification for anthropologists working outside the academy, for example, have met with resistance from both academics and practitioners, although this issue is far from closed.

There is even less consensus within the discipline with regard to those ethical issues that lie squarely outside of the experience of the academic context. Anecdotal evidence indicates that many of the problems faced by practitioners can be significantly different from those faced by their academic colleagues. Practicing anthropologists do research, of course, but they do many other things as well, bringing them into situations largely unfamiliar to their academic colleagues. Barbara Frankel and M. G. Trend insist that "we cannot go on pretending that the problems and predicaments [of academics and practitioners] are identical, or that they can be resolved in the same way for everyone, regardless of the world in which they do their daily work."[14]

## How Is Practice Different?

*Applied anthropology as bad anthropology.* Many academically based anthropologists believe that practice is somehow unethical— that the world of practice contains situations that will compromise anthropologists. Purists within anthropology hold that intervention in the affairs of another culture per se triggers ethical questions, and that intervention only really occurs in situations of practice, not in traditional field research. But practitioners, as Marietta Baba points out,

> often become involved at a field site specifically for the purpose of enabling change through recommendations that emerge from their work. Such conflicts [between traditionalists and practitioners] have prevented anthropology as a whole from embracing and integrating the work of application and practice, and they could cast a shadow over our efforts to move toward greater participation in the policy arena.[15]

In the minds of many critics, there was an age of innocence for anthropology, followed by a fall from grace. Erve Chambers describes the myth in this way:

Once upon a time, anthropologists were of a single mind. They came together in harmony, and agreed on most of the essential points of their profession, including how they should behave in public. This era lasted until quite recently, when there were no longer enough jobs in universities to employ all of our students. These students had to do other things. As we now struggle to accommodate the career needs of these students and former students, we are in danger of jeopardizing the harmony we once enjoyed, even to the point of compromising our ethics.[16]

It is not really surprising that practice has become problematic for some. Anthropology's association with both the Vietnam War and the international development industry has certainly provided the discipline with a few well-documented cases of clear impropriety, together with a vast body of alarming anecdotes (resembling "urban legends") regarding what practitioners may be up to.

Situations of practice, after all, involve anthropologists not so much with poor-but-noble informants, but with actors who have traditionally been viewed with disdain and fear—e.g., government and big business. Practitioners' relationships with these rogues, moreover, appear on occasion to be both lucrative and newsworthy. Berreman comments: "As these corporate and national priorities become anthropologists' priorities, no wonder that the subjects of study no longer come first . . . Anthropologists in these [practitioner] roles are agents of their employers, not advocates for those they study or for the principles of their profession."[17]

On the other side, there is resentment among practitioners toward academics who criticize them without understanding the context in which they work. Hopper, for example, refers pointedly to "the resentment felt by people [i.e., practitioners] scrambling to put food on the table in the rough-and-tumble of the agora, while colleagues quietly petition for grants in the cosseted precincts of the academic hearth."[18]

*How practice differs.*  The ethical issues surrounding practice are immediate, complex, and far-reaching, often quite different from the considerations that come up in research or teaching. Anthropology in application is rarely done for its own sake, but for specific clients, and specific purposes. Practice therefore tends to center on providing clients with insight into how to apply existing anthropological knowledge to a problem and/or generating new knowledge tailored to the client's needs.[19]

The work of practitioners has direct and often immediate effects upon the lives of others, sometimes of great magnitude or significance. Work done outside the academy may be very high-stakes in nature; millions of dollars, hundreds of lives, or thousands of acres may be involved in any decision, and the consequences of that decision may linger for decades.

In the world of practice, knowledge is neither free nor neutral: it is a commodity, valued for its usefulness in achieving some desired result. Because knowledge is valuable, it is subject to various types of control and manipulation that rarely if ever intrude into the academic setting. Because much of the work that practitioners do is client-centered, the nature of the problem—and often, the shape of the preferred solution—have been defined in advance. Client-centered work may inhibit practitioners from investigating things that lie outside the client's interests, or that may conflict with them.

Work funded by a government to produce policy recommendations, for example, is not normally intended to call into question the basic foundations of the entire enterprise. Practitioners, like other specialists, are allowed to criticize and complain a great deal, and are sometimes successful at persuading their employers to see things differently. But one basic rule remains: if persuasion fails, practitioners either fall into line or get out.

"Secrecy" is a complex issue. Knowledge-as-commodity may be withheld, partially or selectively divulged, or willfully misrepresented. As Erve Chambers notes, *all* anthropologists engage in secret research, inasmuch as they decide what to keep and what to discard, what to tell and what to keep silent about. Further, protecting informants' confidentiality is, in effect, a form of secrecy.[20]

Anthropology's professional organizations generally recognize a linked set of domains or stakeholders to whom anthropologists must be responsible. These include: (1) those we study; (2) the public; (3) the discipline; (4) our students; (5) our employers, clients, and sponsors; and (6) governments. Much of the discussion in anthropology regarding ethics has revolved around the priorities and trade-offs to be accorded these different groups.

Although practitioners recognize these six major categories of stakeholders, the practice situation often reveals a much more elaborate cast of actors. Figure 5.4 illustrates some of the kinds of stakeholders likely to be found in any international development project.

**Figure 5.4    Typical Stakeholders in a Development Project**

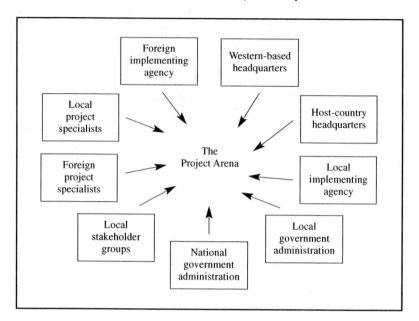

This multiplicity of stakeholders is fairly typical of many of the projects, programs, and activities that practitioners get involved with. Not only will these stakeholders have significantly different needs and expectations at the outset, but these will change and develop over time, as within the complex choreography of a project meanings and arrangements are negotiated and renegotiated.

Real problems arise when obligations to these different groups conflict, as they inevitably will. What happens, for example, when a practitioner learns information that, although privileged, must be made public for the good of another group of stakeholders? We often cannot simply balance these concerns—we must choose one over the other.[21]

Practitioners also face constraints in their work quite different from those that affect their tenured colleagues. To begin with, there is the simple need to make a living. Whereas tenured academics are free to choose their research topics and settings, and to see a project through from start to finish, practitioner participation in a project may be much more piecemeal, and involve much less control and influence. Although in theory practitioners are as free as researchers to pick and choose their areas of engagement, options are not unlimited, and the consequences of choosing one assignment over another are often unclear at the outset.

If practitioners cannot always fully choose what they work on, they are equally constrained as to the use made of the results of their work. What practitioners do is almost certain, much of the time, to have an immediate—as opposed to an eventual, probable, or possible—effect on people's lives. And often, that effect is marked. The knowledge gained by practitioners, and the uses to which that knowledge is put, are most definitely not value-neutral, and there is very little that is "objective" in the process.

Although practitioners must respect confidentiality, as employees they cannot easily refuse to give their clients the information they have been paid to collect. An example of this is the problem of "tacit knowledge"—knowledge that workers in a corporation hold, but that they may not even recognize or express. Baba notes:

> Whether in corporations or in more traditional fieldwork, anthropologists rely on close relationships with key informants. The trust and rapport that ensue can yield information not available to other outsiders. Anthropologists often learn secrets that reveal patterns of human behavior, some of which are illicit. . . .
>
> Anthropologists' ethical duty to protect their informants presents serious challenges inside corporations, particularly when managers ask the researchers to collect workers' informal knowledge. . . .
>
> Anthropologists have ethical obligations to their employers or clients as well as to their informants. Hired to discover information, they cannot simply conceal what they have learned (although withholding data that would harm specific individuals is an accepted practice in anthropology). Nor can they simply walk away from an ethical conflict without running the risk of damaging their careers.[22]

Practitioners are never outside the context of what they do, and they do not have the option of retreating to a tenured position. While "speaking truth to power" is fine in principle, practitioners must always carefully consider the consequences for themselves and other stakeholders.

## Ethics in the Workplace

Although many academic anthropologists consider practice to be ethically suspect, a case might be made for saying that practitioners are often held to higher and closer ethical standards than their university-based counterparts.

In the world of practice, feedback on one's performance usually comes quickly, and the sanctions for unethical behavior are often severe. Judgments about misconduct are usually made by nonanthropologists, using criteria that are often more stringent than those that appear to hold sway within the discipline.

Furthermore, the ethical situations that arise from practice must be actively resolved, not simply avoided, and the consequences of choice for practitioners are usually significant. As a result, practitioners may in many cases be more aware of and sensitive to ethics and ethical nuances than many of their academic colleagues appear to be.

Ethical issues in practice are pervasive, and you will encounter them in your work at a number of levels, on a more or less continuing basis. Some of these will be easy to resolve, others less so. The ethical statements developed within anthropology, while helpful, will have limited applicability much of the time. So here are a few general guidelines for conduct.

Before you accept any practice assignment, make some broad framing decisions about your own values, goals, and comfort level in dealing with certain kinds of stakeholders and problems. If, for example, the ethics of international development planning and practice really bother you on a basic level, then you should probably not be in that business. Similarly, if you fundamentally object to the notion of for-profit corporations, you will do well to stay away from these organizations as clients or colleagues. You do not, in other words, want to put yourself in the position of continually and deeply confronting your own work.

Making these framing choices involves doing two things. The first is clarifying your own personal and professional values, standards, and limits. Know what you can put up with and what you can't, and why. Where are you flexible, and where are you unyielding? This will help you choose where to look for work. The second task involves knowing as much as you can in advance about the nature of the assignment you are being offered. Know the arena you will be operating in, the kinds of people you will be working with, and the types of issues you are likely to encounter.

One writer, for example, divides the ethical choices managers must make into three basic categories:

1. Legal questions: What are the applicable laws or regulations, and should they be obeyed in this instance?
2. Economic and social issues: These generally go beyond the law and relate to cultural values and norms regarding things such as honesty, fairness, and harm. How much consideration should be given to these in this particular instance?
3. One's self-interest: To what extent does your personal well-being come before the interests of other stakeholders in this particular situation?[23]

On the job, work to identify and mobilize sources of support for ethical practice. You are not the only person in the workplace with either an ethical sense or ethical issues to resolve. Devote some time to locating groups and individuals who can help you. These may include people who have had the same or similar types of issues to deal with, as well as people who share your ethical orientation and values.

Ethical guidelines are always partial and incomplete. Use them, but don't expect them to solve problems for you. Your best strategy is to develop an ethical point of view as a practicing anthropologist that is based on the tenets of your discipline—which reflects its ethical standpoint but emanates from who you are and what you value. Own your ethics, in other words. And once you know who you are, ethically speaking, make sure that others know it too.

At the same time, take time to understand the ethical viewpoints and needs of those you work with and work for. These may differ from yours in some respects, but they are likely to coincide in important ways. Differences in viewpoint can often be negotiated, but only if those differences are openly and honestly discussed.

Finally, be flexible where you can. Accommodating your boss, your clients, or your co-workers does not mean that you give away your ability to be both influential and ethical. There are ways of making your point that will, in the long run, do you more good than confrontation. H. Frederick Sweitzer and Mary King suggest a series of steps to deciding dilemmas:

• Identify what you're dealing with: name the problem as explicitly as you can, and focus your attention on the relevant areas. Try to determine what is required in the way of a solution, and within those limits, what your own goals or outcomes should be.

• Do your homework: look at the relevant ethical codes (all of them) to see where the boundaries lie, what the predominant value considerations should be, and whose interests need to be acknowledged. Find past instances of the same problem or issues, and learn about what was done and what effect it had.

• Involve others: consult with your colleagues and your network if possible. They may have valuable experience or insight to share with you about how they handled similar situations. They will also be able to help you brainstorm or strategize about how *you* might react.[24]

As you grope toward an appropriate response, keep some broad questions in mind:

• Is this in the best interests of your client?
• Is anyone likely to be harmed or have their rights violated?
• Is this fair to everyone involved?
• Are you violating any codes or laws?

## Notes

1. See Holton (1998: viii).
2. These principles stem from the work of Robert Chambers (1993, 1997).
3. See Gabarro and Kotter (1980).
4. Fisher and Ury 1981.
5. For more discussion of how to delegate, see Winston (2001: 250–255).
6. For a detailed and very helpful discussion on performance problems and what to do about them, see Mager and Pipe (1970).
7. Stone 1993: 27.
8. See Zey (1984).
9. Kidder 1991: B1.
10. Becker 1986: 28–29.
11. Ervin 2000: 59. Later in the book (pp. 214–217), he provides a helpful section on effective communication for applied anthropologists.
12. Copies of these can be found in the appendix to Fluehr-Lobban 1991: 239–279.

13. Berreman 1991: 53.

14. Frankel and Trend 1991: 180.

15. Baba 1994: 183. In a note, she comments: "'Studying up' in Nader's (1969) sense is quite acceptable, so long as the motive is basic knowledge or better yet, criticism of elites. Working with elites to solve problems often is viewed as unacceptable."

16. Erve Chambers 1991: 170.

17. Berreman 1991: 64.

18. Hopper 1997: 34.

19. See Fluehr-Lobban (1991: 215). See also Gilbert, Tashima, and Fishman (1991: 200); Frankel and Trend (1991); Crain and Tashima (2000).

20. Erve Chambers 1991: 167–168.

21. Fetterman (1983) has discussed two problems that face practitioners particularly. "Guilty knowledge" is confidential knowledge of illegal acts. "Dirty hands" involves not just knowledge of, but participation in, illegal or unethical activity. These situations happen frequently, at a variety of levels, in practice.

22. Baba 1998: B5.

23. See Nash (1993: 5–6) for more discussion.

24. Sweitzer and King 1999:184–186.

# 6

# MAKING IT COUNT:
# ADVANCING THE PROFESSION

In this final chapter, we will look at three broad areas of concern to practitioners. The first of these is the profession of anthropological practice. How can individual practitioners work to build their collective capacity for effective practice? The second area of engagement is that of the discipline of anthropology itself. How can anthropology be redirected to better involve—and respond to—practitioners? The third—and in many ways most important—area is that of the public forum. How can practitioners more effectively contribute to the many important issues that affect our society and others across the globe?

## What Needs Doing?

### The Future of Anthropology

For some time now, we've been engaged in a conversation about where anthropology is likely to go in the future. From this, three possible scenarios have emerged. One is a future where anthropology continues to be more or less what it is today: quaint, interesting, and marginal both inside and outside the academy. A second scenario has anthropology absent altogether: an essentially extinct discipline, having been absorbed, dismantled, or bypassed. The third scenario sees anthropology as a vital contributor to our public intellectual life.[1]

This last may actually be the most likely, for several reasons. One, already noted, is the increasing demand for social knowledge, a demand that cannot be satisfied without the kind of insights that

anthropology provides. As the world globalizes, sociocultural difference is moving in next door, requiring us to make the kinds of public
choices for which anthropology's perspective is uniquely suited.

The second is that, in many ways, anthropology is already an
increasingly influential voice in our public life, thanks in large part
to the efforts of practitioners. For the past several decades, practitioners have worked to define a new kind of anthropology, engaged
with the affairs of the world. Such engagement is unlikely to lessen
in the future.

Today, for these reasons, anthropology students have more
choices about what to do with what they know. To an increasing
extent, they are involving themselves with the great public issues of
our time and finding ways to bring anthropology to bear.

Although the rise of practice has triggered wide and fundamental
changes in anthropology, little of this seems to have been noticed by
the discipline. Twenty years ago, Michael Rynkiewich and James
Spradley commented:

> We are doing all this [work] in anthropology in a planless sort of
> way . . . with no understanding or knowledge of how we are dis-
> tributing manpower in anthropology, and therefore, necessarily no
> understanding of how we should distribute our efforts except
> through rarely voiced but deep prejudices that the best schools
> should concern themselves with the most esoteric work in the most
> ivory tower manner.[2]

This tendency toward muddling through continues today. Leslie
Brownrigg, in a 1997 roundtable conversation in the *Anthropology
Newsletter*,[3] pointed out that the best practitioners have generally
been too busy to interact much with upcoming anthropology students, and that most of what academic anthropologists do is not connected in any significant way to application.

Your contribution as a practitioner will be felt in three main
areas: practice itself, the academy, and society at large. In the rest of
this chapter we'll look at these, one by one.


## Building Practice

### Creating a Profession

A *profession* is an area of practice that encompasses a clearly defined
domain, and applies special knowledge, understanding, and tech-

nique to it. This is done for clients who both value what the profession offers and are willing to pay for that value.[4]

In these terms, anthropology is not yet a profession, and in large measure, this has been our own fault. Although our subject matter—the cultural worlds that humans create and use—is clearly defined, and although our techniques are both unique and insightful, we are still among the most theoretical of disciplines, wary of public engagement.

Until quite recently, discussion of what anthropology is and what it is for was dominated by academicians, who have tended to think of themselves as "the core" and practice as "the periphery."

Controversy continues among academics concerning the proper role of practice and the appropriate status to be accorded practitioners. In the conference halls there is still intense debate over how far anthropology should go in pursuit of public goals, what means and methods should be used, and what roles anthropologists should adopt.

Practitioners, for the most part, have made their peace with issues of engagement. Practitioners now look outside the academy for inspiration, validation, and professional satisfaction. Practitioners are slowly transforming the public face of anthropology into something that looks much more like a profession. To do this, however, they will need to connect more effectively with each other, by creating communities of practice.

## Building Communities of Practice

Establishing strong communities of practice—networks of professionals with shared concerns, issues, and goals who learn from one another—is essential for the advancement of the profession. Although the academic community is characterized by isolated specialists loosely bound through a discipline and interacting as a group only sporadically, practitioners must create more inclusive, collaborative, and proactive communities.

The gains to be realized from the creation of community are enormous, of course. In addition to moral and emotional support, practitioners can use networks to exchange information about methods, findings, and market intelligence.

At the moment, this is not being done in any effective way within the academy, and it will be up to individual practitioners themselves to create and develop effective communities of practice. This can be done in two ways: by establishing personal connections through mentoring, and by developing wider networks.

The creation of professional spaces where practitioners can talk to each other has already begun, but must be extended and expanded. Such networks can also perform a very valuable training function. Through the collection and exchange of the lessons of experience, practitioners not only strengthen their own capacities, but help build it among those just entering the profession.

*Mentoring younger professionals.*   As a practitioner, it is very important for you to establish working connections with younger practitioners, for several reasons. For one thing, there is no well-established mechanism for easing entry for younger anthropologists into the field of practice. Because of the poorly articulated links that most anthropology programs have with the world outside the academy, each graduating cohort is essentially on its own.

By serving as a mentor for younger graduates, you can help connect them with others in their chosen field, and provide them with valuable career advice based on your own experience. You can also offer criticism, feedback, and suggestions on their own work.

If you have the type of job that allows you to offer internships, practicums, or consultancies to outsiders, consider making these available to recent graduates. Developing mentoring and advising relationships with individual practitioners, although time-consuming, is an excellent way to help bring the benefits of your work and experience to others.

*Creating professional networks.*   Whether or not you develop mentoring relationships with individual practitioners, you should work to create and extend networks. Local practitioner organizations are one very good way to network. If an LPO does not exist in your area, consider setting one up. LPOs and larger professional associations—AAA, NAPA, and SfAA in particular—can be vehicles for organizing training events focused on practitioner issues. Serving on various committees in these professional organizations is also a good way to network.

The Web now makes it easy to locate other professionals and to discuss issues with them. There are now an impressive number of websites and bulletin boards of interest to practitioners.

### Developing a Theory of Practice

A "theory of practice" refers to an overarching set of propositions and principles serving to explain and guide the application of anthropology to real-life situations. As William A. Partridge pointed out some time ago, anthropology has been hampered by the lack of such a theory, and few attempts have been made within the academy to develop one.[5]

In many ways this is not surprising, given the academy's ambivalence toward practice and its general unfamiliarity with the conditions and situations that constrain and guide how practitioners work. It will therefore fall to practitioners themselves to develop and elaborate an explicit theory of practice.

One important aspect of this will be the investigation of practice as a form of artistry, as a continuing dialogue between the practitioner and the situation of practice. Understanding how the architecture of discourse between practitioners and the environment is constructed, maintained, and/or altered will help us develop a theory of practice that is both intellectually sound and practically relevant. We will need to identify different forms of this dialogue and examine their relative effectiveness. We also need to understand the factors that can interfere with the development of professional artistry.

*A literature of practice.* One way to do this is to develop a specific literature of practice. Despite all that has been written on anthropology, applied anthropology, and practice, we really know very little—in an ethnographic sense—about how practitioners actually do their work on a day-to-day basis.

Most practitioners work in situations of planned change, at one level or another. And most understand that they are part of a context encompassing place, people, and project, where understanding, meanings, and outcomes unfold over time as part of a complex process of negotiation. One observer characterized the process as "a messy business . . . a negotiated, socially constructed, never-ending interaction between many social actors."[6]

If practice is a negotiation, where the participants eventually come to terms, we lack an in-depth understanding of how and why this happens in specific instances. To advance practice, we need to understand how meanings are created in practice situations, and how they change over time in response to events.

Each situation of practice, no matter how small, is an experiment to see how anthropology can be applied to a particular context. A literature of practice will help us understand how anthropologists in these situations frame their problems and work with others to achieve satisfactory outcomes.

*Ethics for the real world.* Practitioners will also need to generate an authentic ethics of practice that helps them navigate the complexities of the multiple worlds they work in, and that originates from the experiences of those worlds, rather than emanating from what are essentially academic issues and concerns.

It has been clear for some time that the existing ethical codes within anthropology are inadequate to guide practice. They are not so much wrong as partial, for the situations that practitioners encounter are almost always more diverse, more complex, and more troubling than the academy has ever explicitly recognized.

One of the greatest contributions that practitioners will be able to make to anthropology is therefore the development of an ethics of practice to inform the present and guide the future.

*Standards.*  Finally, practitioners will have to define and develop standards for acceptable practice. The issue of standards or certification has been debated—sometimes hotly—several times within the discipline in the last several decades, without concrete result.

Sooner or later, part of making anthropology a profession will involve creating—and enforcing—professional standards for practitioners. Up until now, the academy has always assumed that it alone would determine what those standards should be. It is certainly true, of course, that whatever standards are adopted must find direct expression through the content of academic programs. But standards *for* practice, to be relevant, must arise directly *from* the experience of practice itself.

Practitioners will therefore have to begin to develop standards that realistically reflect the demands and expectations of their jobs, and they must engage in constructive dialogue with their academic colleagues about how these standards will be introduced into anthropological training.


## Redirecting the Discipline

Today, the academy is disconnected from practice in significant ways. To some extent, it can be argued that the current split between academically oriented and practice-oriented anthropologists is a mutually convenient way of allowing each to do more or less as they please.[7]

But to permit this situation to continue indefinitely would put both academic anthropology and practice at risk. There is an urgent need for practitioners to reach out to their academic colleagues, and to work with them to reform the content and thrust of anthropological training. This will require the academy to learn more about not only how practice is done, but also about how it can be taught. But it will also require practitioners to produce more and better work of the type that lends itself to university teaching.

Linking theory and practice more closely within the academy will have political implications for the academy and its institutional culture. Ernest Boyer, who wrote extensively on the role and mission of the university in today's society, believed in the "scholarship of application" and felt strongly that it should have equal place in the academy beside the scholarship of discovery—i.e., research.[8]

But much research today is essentially irrelevant to the concerns of the wider society, unless one argues, as some do, that "theory separated from practice, critique without action, and academic pyrotechnics" exist mainly in order to serve the purposes of large and powerful societal interests.[9]

## Redirecting Anthropology

The task here is essentially that of redirecting academic anthropology, orienting it more toward serving the needs of practitioners *and* prospective academics.

In terms of the extent to which anthropological training prepares graduates for the world of practice, and in terms of the extent to which anthropology as a discipline learns from the world of practice, little has changed in the past three decades. Although there are now several dozen training programs in North America, we still do not have anything resembling a true professional school focused on the needs of practitioners.

Training for anthropologists has traditionally emphasized skills that prepare them for academic careers. But practice—as we have seen—requires skills, knowledge, and approaches that extend beyond the traditional four-field boundaries of the discipline, even as the processes and products of practice remain uniquely anthropological.

Even today, most traditional anthropology departments hardly recognize the existence of a market for their students outside of academic employment itself. And if members of the academy do sometimes acknowledge the presence of the market, they do not necessarily see it as their job to prepare students for it in any way other than to show them how to become professors like themselves.

Few anthropology departments invest time and resources in publicizing jobs in practice or in tracking their graduates' careers in practice. Few have established strong links with those sectors and industries that employ practitioners. And few have mechanisms in place to use feedback from these employers—or from practitioners themselves—to improve the training they offer.

Changing the orientation of our anthropology departments is necessary if only because it is what students so clearly need. But what students need is also connected to a broader, longer-term issue, and that is the survival of the discipline itself. As several observers have commented, the fate of academic departments of anthropology is increasingly linked to the success of practitioners outside the academy.[10]

## Bringing Practice In

One way to change the character of academic anthropology is to bring practitioners into the training process. Here again, only a few departments do this to any appreciable extent. But it seems obvious that to educate the next generation of practitioners, we will need to provide them with role models.

Most of the anthropologists engaged in full-time practice—in some cases for decades—have had neither the time nor the opportunity to share their experiences and insights with the academy. This tends to perpetuate a situation in which each succeeding cohort of practitioner anthropologists finds itself essentially unprepared for the world outside the university, and where each cohort must learn, not from their professors, but from each other.

Although individual anthropology professors may recognize the value of involving practitioners with their departments, the departments themselves may not. Because the barriers to promoting effective practice outside the academy stem largely (though not exclusively) from the structure, content, and philosophy of university training, these same things tend to mitigate against practitioner involvement with that training.

The advantages of practitioner involvement are evident. Academics and practitioners can both benefit from intellectual cross-fertilization. Students will benefit, too; in addition to learning *what* practitioners do, they will have the opportunity to hear them explain *why* and *how* they do their work as they do. The issue of anthropology's relation to the world at large can be addressed through courses, but it is through relationships with flesh-and-blood practitioners that the issue becomes real.

Bringing practitioners into the academy may require rethinking tenure, research, and publication arrangements, and creating special positions for practitioners of both a temporary and a full-time nature.

## Connecting with the Academy

There are many ways for you, as a practitioner, to become involved with academic training programs. Here are some of the main options.

*Guest lectures.* Almost all anthropology departments will be happy to invite you to present your work to faculty or to give a lecture to students in an applied course. In many cases, they will be prepared to pay you an honorarium for this. Whether or not you actually get paid for your appearances, this is an excellent chance to showcase your work and to understand more about what students and their instructors are doing.

*Teaching.* Opportunities for part-time teaching in anthropology abound in most institutions. Anthropology remains a popular undergraduate choice for many, and this fact, coupled with the recurring need to find replacements for faculty who are on leave, on sabbatical, or burdened with administrative duties, creates a ready market.

Adjunct teaching stipends won't even begin to pay your bills, but there are other rewards for teaching. As all teachers discover, the best way to learn something—or to learn it better—is to teach it to others, and the experience of explaining yourself to a class of students will stimulate and energize you as it causes you to reflect.

The resources of even the most modest universities are impressive, and as an adjunct, these will be at your disposal. Internet access, library access, office space, and possibly even research or teaching assistance can be yours for a term or two, as you teach your courses.

The main reward, of course, is the chance to connect with students—to present anthropological practice to them in ways that inform and excite them about the possibilities for using what they learn outside the academy.

*Advising and mentoring.* Whether or not you choose to teach, you can advise and mentor students in various ways. Here again, this is a wonderful opportunity to establish ties to both students and departments, and to provide a practitioner's perspective.

In some programs, the regular academic advising load is so heavy that departments seek outside help. Other departments sometimes engage outsiders to help read student reports and papers.

Most academic programs require graduate students to have one or more outside members on their thesis committees, and these can include practitioners. If you have the chance, you should definitely offer to serve on such committees. You will not only gain valuable insight into how students are advised, guided, and evaluated within a particular institution, but more importantly, you will be able to influence that process.

Some departments have started mentoring programs to connect students with working professionals outside the department. If you are lucky enough to have one of these programs in your vicinity, this is an excellent way to establish a connection with your academic peers and with students.

*Internships.* Today, more and more applied-anthropology programs recognize that they must provide their students with opportunities to learn outside the classroom. Increasingly, students themselves demand such opportunities. Offering to arrange internships for students will earn you the gratitude and respect of people in the department, while giving you a chance to show students how anthropology can be used in the workplace.

*Advisory boards and committees.* There may be opportunities to connect with the university through membership on committees, boards, or other groups. Programs often have advisory boards, for example, that include outside professionals. They may also have a board of visitors, which functions somewhat like an accrediting body. Or they may have other committees or working groups to help them with aspects of program planning, curriculum, or evaluation.

In any of these cases, your input as a practicing professional may be welcomed. Your experience outside the academy will be very valuable to faculty as they seek to improve their programs, and in turn, you will gain insight into how students might be better prepared for careers in practice.

*Joint projects and activities.*   You can also seek opportunities to connect with academic colleagues on matters of mutual interest. Faculty sometimes have research projects that can utilize outside specialists. Often, however, it is you who have research or consulting assignments to offer to the faculty. Alternatively, you may find that you share an interest in some community issue with one or more members of the faculty. Working together with an academic colleague on such issues is, again, an opportunity for cross-fertilization.

In some cases, you may want to join with faculty in writing for publication, either in academic journals or for a wider audience. Working with your academic colleagues on articles, books, or reports is an excellent way for you to build a better appreciation for teamwork, while allowing you to combine your perspectives with those of others to produce work that extends your reach.

*Local practitioner organizations.*   Finally, don't forget LPOs, whose membership in many locations is predominantly academic. Becoming active in an LPO is an excellent way to connect with your academic counterparts, and to exchange views and information with them. A group that includes both academics and outside practitioners can be an excellent forum for discussion about the differences between academic anthropology and practice, as well as a way to focus on common concerns.

## Engaging the Public

### Building an Anthropology of Engagement

To paraphrase another writer, we have somehow managed, within anthropology, to construct a discipline in which the connections are largely missing between some of our best minds and some of our society's most pressing problems.[11]

Both intellectually and as a practical matter, anthropology needs to be more involved with public life. We must not only attempt to understand the world, but to engage with it, and change it where necessary. And this requires the active participation of both theorists and practitioners. Anthropology, as Erve Chambers reminds us, is more than a science; it is a form of participation in human affairs.[12]

But anthropology cannot contribute effectively to the public dialogue unless it is willing to roll up its sleeves and enter public life. Although anthropologists are still studying up, increasing numbers of practitioners are now "moving up" into positions of influence and authority. As they do, anthropology becomes both more visible and more integral to problem solving. Alfred Hess states the need clearly: "If we want to be more fully represented in the body politic, we have to be willing to become a part of that culture. When we do, we will be called upon and consulted because of our experience in policy setting, not because we are anthropologists. But in that process, anthropology will have gained a wider voice."[13]

It is through engagement, not through detachment, that anthropological practice will find its true professional identity and its authentic public voice. Action does not challenge anthropology's traditional role—it extends it.

It has been fashionable in anthropology for too long to be disengaged from the world, to pretend to be above the mess and the fray. But as we participate and engage, we acquire new skills and strength. To continually feel that we don't know enough, that we don't have enough influence, or that we might be wrong is to condemn ourselves to roles of immobility and irrelevance. Being perfect probably isn't possible in most cases. Being authentic is what is important.

In our efforts to improve society, we will of course join with others. We improve our practice and strengthen our discipline by interacting with groups outside our own professional communities. If we only talk to those who already understand—and agree with—us, we will learn little, and contribute even less.

Our most pressing human problems are common problems, and they can only be resolved through common effort. But anthropology has a distinctive contribution to make: we are good at what Wendell Berry calls "solving for pattern"—situating a solution within its overall context in such a way that change does not ignore or disregard the larger connections of which it is a part.[14]

This effort to bring anthropology more fully into our public life will be a long-term process, extending beyond any single person's professional life. As the political journalist I. F. Stone remarked, "If you expect to see the final results of your work, you simply have not asked a big enough question."[15]

## Telling Your Story

If we are to have wide impact on the public dialogue, anthropology needs much more visibility. As Ralph Bishop once noted, Margaret Mead dead is better journalistic copy than most living anthropologists.[16]

If, as a practitioner, you believe that you have things to say that are worth hearing, you need to go public with them. And to do this, you need to make a serious commitment to public writing and public speaking.

*Overcome your modesty.* As anthropologists, we're often far too modest about our accomplishments. We're trained to specialize, and we're warned not to intrude on other specialists' areas. We're definitely not encouraged to popularize what we know by writing for a general audience.

Fortunately, practitioners are less susceptible to these traps than academic anthropologists, for a variety of reasons. First of all, the very nature of their work forces practitioners to work and think outside their comfort zone much of the time, and to develop a broad-based, holistic view of what they're doing.

Second, practitioners work with a variety of others in virtually all situations of practice. Some of them may be anthropologists, but most of them will not be. Practitioners are accustomed to having to defend and justify what they think and do, and they are equally used to questioning the assumptions and methods of others. This gives practitioners a direct understanding of how different disciplines and approaches work together—or fail to work together—to produce results.

Third, practitioners deal less with abstract theory and more with the everyday concerns of real people. Issues and ideas are debated in the public forum, where everyone has a voice, not just the experts, and where everyone is to some extent affected by the outcomes. Practitioners learn to present their thoughts and findings to this wider audience in terms that are persuasive, illuminating, and intelligible.

So it's not just permissible for practitioners to tell their stories and share their thoughts; it's a requirement. Assuming that you have things to say, then, how should you go about saying them?

*Keep a record.*   Become your own archivist. Your thoughts will develop over time, and you will find yourself generating fresh insights regarding material you've already worked on. Keep copies of everything that you produce. This includes not only reports, articles, and analyses related to your work, but talks and presentations you give—in short, anything you produce that is an expression of your professional work. Keep a file, too, of anything written about you or your work.

Telling your story will be done in different ways at different times to different audiences. Having a comprehensive set of records will help you understand how your ideas have progressed, how they've been expressed in the past, and how they might be further shaped in the future. No body of work is ever finished.

*Connect your work to that of others.*   Like other academic specialists, anthropologists are trained to be individual thinkers and researchers, to work largely in isolation from their colleagues. As we've seen, however, the world of practice requires teamwork, often among people with very different backgrounds. John van Willigen reminds us that there are really no such things as anthropological problems—there are only client problems.[17]

Teamwork is an excellent way to gain perspective on what you know. In some cases, collaboration will help you distinguish your approach from that of others. At the same time, you'll find that your own ideas are considerably enhanced and extended through contact with what others think. And you may often find that it's easier to get a hearing for your views if they are combined with those of others.

*Get it out the door.*   Once you have something to say, seek every opportunity to get into print. You should be publishing as often as you can, in as many different ways as you can.

There are many publishing outlets for someone with something to say. In addition to the academic presses, there are trade publishers—both general and specialized—as well as journals, newspapers, university centers, and an enormous variety of civic and professional societies, all of which publish.

Publishing serves multiple purposes for practitioners: it helps educate the public and policymakers about what anthropology does, how it works, and what it contributes. It also creates useful materials for training younger practitioners.

Mitchell Allen of AltaMira Press reminds us that good professional writing is immediate, problem-specific, concise, and action-oriented.[18] It explains things to readers in terms that are clear and compelling. Some of the most persuasive writing achieves its impact because it presents new information to people, but is framed within the context of values, hopes, and concerns that they already have. And some of the best writing is unabashedly partisan.[19]

Consider public speaking as well as writing. The AAA and the SfAA meetings are excellent places to present, but you have many other nonacademic opportunities to speak available to you. Every town of a respectable size will have its service clubs, voluntary associations, and educational institutions, and these are superb opportunities to get your message out.

## Conclusion: Getting Down to Work

In 1987, Erve Chambers warned: "The lack of development of a practitioner arm in anthropology does not ensure the purity of the anthropological enterprise so much as it guarantees that the knowledge of anthropology will be little used and that, when it is used, it is likely to be misused."[20]

Fortunately, anthropological practice *has* developed, and today is clearly coming into its own. As members of a rapidly evolving profession, practitioners have demonstrated their ability to contribute positively and innovatively to the public dialogue.

Although anthropological practice is thriving, there is more to be done: our global problems cry out for the kinds of understanding that anthropology seems best suited to provide. Providing this effectively, however, will mean moving to the next level: building a profession of practice that is closely linked to a progressive, outward-looking discipline. If anthropology can do this, it has the opportunity to make a major contribution to constructing our collective future.

This will require from us clear engagement, teamwork, a willingness to learn from others, risk taking, and above all, a commitment to change—all things that, traditionally, our discipline has for the most part carefully avoided. Fortunately, practitioners have shown us the way.

The future presents us with enormous challenges and opportunities. Anthropology can play a central and critical role in meeting these challenges, but only if anthropologists themselves—practitioners and academics—are equal to the task. Robert Hackenberg urges younger anthropologists: "Now as you start to focus your telescopes on the forbidding landscape before you, steady your hand with the knowledge that you stand in the shadow of the giants of the past. You are descended from a family of living legends. This is *your* turn to add *your* chapter."[21]

Anthropology could choose, of course, to remain outside the fray. We could choose to remain within the institutions and conceptual frameworks that are most familiar to us, gazing critically out at the world but never quite daring to fully enter the arena, to raise our voices, or to extend our hands to others.

We could always do that. For as they say, a ship is safe in its harbor.

But that's not what ships are for.

## Notes

1. See Peacock (1999: 25).
2. Rynkiewich and Spradley 1981: 179–180.
3. In Joseph (1997: 11).
4. See Greenwood (1957) for more discussion.
5. Partridge 1985.
6. Pottier 1993b: 27–28.
7. Greenwood 2000: 168.
8. Coye 1997: 22.
9. Greenwood 2000: 174.
10. Johnsrud 2000: 248.
11. Kidder 1991: B1.
12. Erve Chambers 1985: 189.
13. Hess 1993: 48.
14. In Loeb (1999: 130).
15. Ibid., p. 114.
16. Bishop 1985: 18.
17. Van Willigen 1986: 215.
18. Mitchell Allen, in Puntenny (1991: 25–26).
19. See Hackenberg (1999).
20. Erve Chambers 1987: 325.
21. Hackenberg 1988: 184.

# APPENDIX: RESOURCES FOR FURTHER LEARNING

The literature of practice is expanding rapidly, and websites proliferate (and change addresses) even more rapidly. The following resources are but a sample of what is available.

## Applied and Practice-Oriented Anthropology Programs in North America

The following list appears on the SfAA website (http://www.sfaa.net/) and the Applied Anthropology Computer Network (ANTHAP) website (http://anthap.oakland.edu/gradprog.htm). All of the anthropology programs listed here have websites of their own, and many of these offer links to other anthropology resources.

You can find the home pages of virtually any university or college in North America and many other places in the world at the following website: http://www.mit.edu:8001/people/cdemello/univ.html.

Arizona
    Northern Arizona University
    University of Arizona
California
    California State University, Chico
    California State University, Long Beach
    University of California, San Francisco

Connecticut
  University of Connecticut
District of Columbia
  American University
  Catholic University of America
  The George Washington University
  The George Washington University, Elliott School of International Affairs
Florida
  Florida State University
  University of Florida
  University of Miami
  University of South Florida
Georgia
  Georgia State University
  University of Georgia
Indiana
  University of Indianapolis
Kansas
  University of Kansas
Kentucky
  Northern Kentucky University
  University of Kentucky
Louisiana
  University of New Orleans
Maryland
  University of Maryland, College Park
Massachusetts
  Boston University
Michigan
  Michigan State University
  Wayne State University
Mississippi
  Mississippi State University
New Jersey
  Montclair State College
New York
  State University of New York, Binghamton
  State University of New York, Buffalo
  Teacher's College, Columbia University

Ontario
    York University
Oregon
    Oregon State University
Quebec
    McGill University
Tennessee
    University of Memphis
Texas
    Southern Methodist University
    University of North Texas

## Professional Organizations

### National Organizations

- Society for Applied Anthropology: http://www.sfaa.net/
- American Anthropological Association: http://www.aaanet.org/
- National Association for the Practice of Anthropology: http://www.aaanet.org/napa/
- National Association of Student Anthropologists: http://www.aaanet.org/nasa/
- Society for Applied Anthropology: http://www.sfaa.net/
- High Plains Society for Applied Anthropology: http://www.hpsfaa.org/

APA's website provides information on the NAPA Mentor Program, which offers career assistance to anthropology students and anthropologists in career transition. The NAPA Bulletin Series is described (along with other useful links) at: http://www.NAPA Bulletin.org/.

### Local Practitioner Organizations

A list of LPOs can be found on the NAPA website: http://www.aaanet.org/napa/. Active LPOs include these:
    Chicago Association for Practicing Anthropologists
    Great Lakes Association of Practicing Anthropologists
    Mid-South Association of Practicing Anthropologists

North Florida Network of Practicing Anthropologists
Philadelphia Association of Practicing Anthropologists
Southern California Applied Anthropology Network
Sun Coast Organization of Practicing Anthropologists (SCOPA)
Washington Association of Professional Anthropologists
(WAPA). One of the largest and oldest LPOs, WAPA has its own
website at: http://www.smcm.edu/wapa/.
Some background on LPOs can be found in the following publications:

Bainton, Barry. 1979. "SOPA: Cultivating the Profession and
  Harvesting at the Grassroots Level," *Human Organization*
  38, no. 3: 318–319.

Bennett, Linda A. 1988. *Bridges for Changing Times: Local
  Practitioner Organizations in American Anthropology*,
  NAPA Bulletin No. 6, Washington, DC, American
  Anthropological Association.

Fiske, Shirley, and Erve Chambers. 1996. "The Inventions of
  Practice," *Human Organization* 55, no. 1 (spring): 1–12.

## Other Practitioner Organizations

Several anthropology-based private firms also maintain useful websites of interest to practitioners. Some of these websites contain job
announcements from time to time. Among them are:
The Context-Based Research Group in Baltimore:
    http://www.contextresearch.com/context/
    They also have a website specifically for jobs at:
    http://www.anthrojob.com/
LTG Associates is an anthropological consulting firm, with
offices in Turlock, CA, and Washington, DC. Their website is:
    http://www.ltgassociates.com/
The Center for Anthropology and Science Communication
(CASC), in Washington, DC, maintains a website at:
    http://sciencesitescom.com/CASC/
Ethnographic Research Inc:
    http://www.ethnographic-research.com/
Practical Gatherings, based in Half Moon Bay, CA, is one of the
first "communities of practice." It is a division of Social
Solutions Inc., a firm specializing in workplace anthropology.

Their website contains a number of useful sections and links:

http://www.practicalgatherings.com/

## Other Resources for Practitioners

• NAPA Bulletins: This extremely useful series is available to NAPA members. The website describing the series (with other useful links) is at: http://www.napabulletin.org/.

• *Anthropologists at Work: Careers Making a Difference*: This 36-minute VHS video highlights the work of several applied anthropologists. It is available from the American Anthropological Association, 4350 North Fairfax Dr., Suite 640, Arlington, VA 22203, (703) 528-1902, x3004.

• The quarterly journal *Practicing Anthropology* has been the major resource in the past several decades for students wishing to enter practice, offering articles from anthropologists working in a wide variety of fields. You can look at the contents of the current issue at: http://www.sfaa.net/pa/pa.html.

## Anthropology-Related Websites

### Anthropology in the News

The work of practitioners is often featured in major news stories. Several useful websites that link to anthropology in the national media would include these:

• Context-Based Research: http://www.contextresearch.com/context/
• Texas A&M University: http://www.tamu.edu/anthropology/news.html

### Applied- and Practice-Oriented Anthropology Websites

• ANTHAP, the Applied Anthropology Computer Network, maintains a comprehensive and highly informative website at http://anthap.oakland.edu.

The ANTHAP site has extensive links to other sites. Of these, three are particularly important:

• The Applied Anthropology Documentation Project at the University of Kentucky, which contains reports, proposals, conference papers, and other "grey literature" produced by practicing and applied anthropologists.
• NAPA's "Guidelines for Training Practicing Anthropologists," developed by NAPA and the SfAA, which provides guidelines for the design and administration of degree-granting graduate training.
• A list of graduate programs in applied anthropology (see above) with direct links to many program home pages: http://anthap. oakland.edu/gradprog.htm.

AnthroTech, which is actually a Web development service, also has an extensive array of Web-based services for practitioners, including career information, discussion forums, job postings, and links to other sites, such as the WWW Virtual Library: http://www. anthrotech.com/. For the WWW Virtual Library alone: http://vlib. anthrotech.com/.

Several publishers have websites on anthropology that include sections on applied and practice matters:

• Wadsworth Publishing's website contains a section on anthropology careers: http://www.wadsworth.com/anthropology_d/ resources/exchange/careers.html.
And one on anthropology in business: http://www.wadsworth. com/anthropology_d/resources/exchange/business.html.
• Harcourt Brace Publishers also has a useful website on anthropology, with links and career advice: http://www.harbrace. com/anthro/.

Other useful sites for practitioners would include these:

• Nicole's Anthro Page. This site contains numerous links to other sites of interest to practitioners: http://www.wsu.edu/~ i9248809/anthrop.html.
• The Worldwide Email Directory of Anthropologists (WEDA). This site will enable you to find and contact thousands of anthropolo-

gists around the world: http://wings.buffalo.edu/academic/department/anthropology/weda/.

- Two surveys of graduate education, while not focused specifically on anthropology, contain very interesting information for anyone contemplating a Ph.D. program. The first, the 2000 National Doctoral Program Survey, was carried out by the National Association of Graduate-Professional Students. The website can be found at: http://survey.nagps.org/.

- The second survey on Doctoral Education and Career Preparation was done by the Pew Charitable Trusts in 2001. Their website contains sections on how to choose a program, and should definitely be consulted before you enter a program. The website can be found at: http://www.wcer.wisc.edu/phd-survey/.

Other Internet resources for practitioners are listed in the *Anthropology Newsletter* (January 1998): 25.

## Job and Career Websites

There are numerous websites offering advice and information about career planning, as well as actual job postings. I have included only a few of the more well-known ones here. A little time spent online will turn up dozens more.

## General Job and Career Links

- http://www.headhunter.net/
- http://careers.yahoo.com/
- http://www.hotjobs.com/
- http://www.nonprofitjobs.org/
- http://www.idealist.org/
- www.studentjobs.gov
- http://www.jobstar.org
- http://www.wetfeet.com/asp/home.asp
- http://goodworksfirst.org/
- http://www.nonprofitjobs.org/
- http://joboptions.careers.flipdog.com/
- http://www.monster.com/
- http://www.salary.com

About.com has a variety of pages on jobs, career planning, and job hunting, both domestic and international: http://about.com/.

The *Chronicle of Higher Education* has an extensive collection

of articles and data on jobs for M.A.s and Ph.D.s, including nonacademic jobs. Some of their links are for subscribers only, but most are
free, at: http://chronicle.com. Their extensive archives section also
includes a series on anthropology: http://chronicle.com/jobs/archive/
topical/anthropology.htm.

## Links Relating to Overseas Jobs

Since many practitioners work overseas, here are some sites focused
on nonprofit, development-oriented, and humanitarian work in
other countries. Again, this is only a sample of the many sites in existence.

- NGO Worldline is a comprehensive website on nonprofits:
  http://www.sover.net/~paulven/ngo.html.
- A comprehensive directory of development organizations can
  be found here: http://www.devdir.org/.
- International, nonprofit, humanitarian, and development-
  related jobs can be found at: http://www.oneworld.org/
  jobs/.
- Interaction, a coalition of U.S.-based nonprofits, has a website at: http://www.interaction.org/.
- Volunteers in Technical Assistance has a website at:
  http://www.vita.org/.
- Another list of international NGOs is provided by the United
  Nations, at: http://www.un.org/MoreInfo/ngolink/ngodir.htm.
- Monster.com has a section of its website devoted to international jobs: http://international.monster.com/.
- The International Jobs Center has a website listing a variety
  of development-oriented jobs overseas: http://www.
  internationaljobs.org/.

## Job Links for Anthropologists

- The Context-Based Research Group has jobs on its website:
  http://www.anthrojob.com/.
- Northern Kentucky University has a wonderful website on
  anthropology, including a very helpful section on "careers":
  http://www.nku.edu/~anthro/careers.html.

# Print Resources

## Books and Monographs on Applied Anthropology and Practice

Arensberg, Conrad M., and Arthur H. Niehoff. 1964. *Introducing Social Change: A Manual for Americans Overseas*, Chicago, Aldine Publishing Company.

Belshaw, Cyril S. 1976. *The Sorcerer's Apprentice: An Anthropology of Public Policy*, New York, Pergamon.

Chambers, Erve. 1985. *Applied Anthropology: A Practical Guide*, Prospect Heights, IL, Waveland Press.

Eddy, Elizabeth M., and William L. Partridge. 1978. *Applied Anthropology in America*, New York, Columbia University Press.

Ervin, Alexander. 2000. *Applied Anthropology: Tools and Perspectives for Contemporary Practice*, Boston, Allyn & Bacon.

Foster, G. M. 1969. *Applied Anthropology*, Boston, Little, Brown and Company Inc.

Goodenough, Ward H. 1963. *Cooperation in Change*, New York, Russell Sage Foundation.

Hill, Carole E., and Marietta L. Baba (eds.) 2000. *The Unity of Theory and Practice in Anthropology: Rebuilding a Fractured Synthesis*, NAPA Bulletin #18, Washington, DC, American Anthropological Association.

Paul, Benjamin D. (ed.). 1955. *Health, Culture, and Community: Case Studies of Public Reactions to Health Programs*, New York, Russell Sage Foundation.

Spicer, Edward (ed.). 1952. *Human Problems in Technological Change*, New York, Russell Sage Foundation.

Trotter, R. (ed.). 1988. *Anthropology for Tomorrow*, AAA/NAPA Publication No. 24, Washington, DC, American Anthropological Association.

van Willigen, John. 1986. *Applied Anthropology: An Introduction*, South Hadley, MA, Bergin & Garvey.

van Willigen, John. 1991. *Anthropology in Use: A Source Book on Anthropological Practice*, Westview Special Studies in Applied Anthropology, Boulder, CO, Westview Press.

van Willigen, John. 1993. *Applied Anthropology* (revised edition), South Hadley, MA, Bergin & Garvey.

Wulff, R. M., and S. J. Fiske (eds.) 1987. *Anthropological Praxis: Translating Knowledge into Action*, Boulder, CO, Westview Press.

## Books and Articles on Aspects of Graduate School

Anderson, Geoff, David Boud, and Jane Sampson. 1996. *Learning Contracts: A Practical Guide*, London, Kogan Page Limited.

Angrosino, Michael V. 1981. "Practicum Training in Applied Anthropology," *Human Organization* 40, no. 1: 81–84.

Arcieri, Anthony J., and Marianne Green. 2000. *Majoring in Success: Building Your Career While Still in College*, Alexandria, VA, Octameron Associates.

Clark, Robert E., and John Palattella (eds.). 1997. *The Real Guide to Grad School: What You Better Know Before You Choose Humanities and Social Sciences*, New York, Lingua Franca.

Green, Marianne Ehrlich. 1997. *Internship Success*, Lincolnwood, IL, VGM Career Horizons.

Hyland, Stanley, and Sean Kirkpatrick. 1989. *Guide to Training Programs in Applied Anthropology*, Memphis, TN, Society for Applied Anthropology.

Mitchell, Lesli. 1996. *The Ultimate Grad School Survival Guide*, Paterson, NJ, Peterson's.

Oldman, Mark, and Samer Hamadeh. 2002. *The Internship Bible 2002*, New York, Princeton Review.

Peters, Robert L. 1992. *Getting What You Came For*, New York, Farrar, Straus, and Giroux.

Peterson's Guides. 2001. *Peterson's Internships 2002*, Princeton, NJ, Peterson's Guides.

Schön, Donald. 1983. *The Reflective Practitioner: How Professionals Think in Action*, New York, Basic Books.

Schön, Donald. 1987. *Educating the Reflective Practitioner: Toward a New Design for Teaching and Learning in the Professions*, San Francisco, Jossey-Bass.

Shields, Charles J. 1994. *Back in School: A Guide for Adult Learners*, Hawthorne, NJ, Career Press.

Sweitzer, H. Frederick, and Mary A. King. 1999. *The Successful Internship*, Pacific Grove, CA, Brooks/Cole Publishing.

## Books on Career Planning and Job Hunting

American Anthropological Association. 1982. *Getting a Job Outside the Academy*, Washington, DC, American Anthropological Association.

Basalla, Susan, and Maggie Debelius. 2001. *"So What Are You Going to Do with That?": A Guide to Career-Changing for M.A.'s and Ph.D.'s*, New York, Farrar, Straus, and Giroux.

Basch, Linda G., Lucie Wood Saunders, Jagna Wojcicka Sharff, and James Peacock (eds.). 1999. *Transforming Academia: Challenges and Opportunities for an Engaged Anthropology*, American Ethnological Society Monograph Series No. 8, Washington, DC, American Anthropological Association.

Birkel, J. Damien, and Stacey J. Miller. 1998. *Career Bounce-Back!* New York, American Management Association.

Bolles, Richard. 1978. *The Three Boxes of Life*, Berkeley, CA, Ten Speed Press.

Bolles, Richard. 2001. *What Color Is Your Parachute?* Berkeley, CA, Ten

Speed Press.

Bridges, William. 1991. *Managing Transitions: Making the Most of Change*, Reading, MA, Addison-Wesley.

Camenson, Blythe. 2000. *Great Jobs for Anthropology Majors*, Lincolnwood, IL, VGM Career Horizons.

Cohen, Lilly, and Dennis R. Young. 1989. *Careers for Dreamers and Doers: A Guide to Management Careers in the Nonprofit Sector*, New York, The Foundation Center.

Everett, Melissa. 1995. *Making a Living While Making a Difference: A Guide to Creating Careers with a Conscience*, New York, Bantam Books.

Falvey, Jack. 1987. *What's Next: Career Strategies After 35*, Charlotte, VT, Williamson Publishing.

Hanna, Sharon L. 1998. *Career Development by Design*, Upper Saddle River, NJ, Prentice-Hall.

Hansen, L. Sunny. 1997. *Integrative Life Planning*, San Francisco, Jossey-Bass.

Hanson, Karen J. (ed.). 1988. *Mainstreaming Anthropology: Experiences in Government Employment*, NAPA Bulletin No. 5, Washington, DC, American Anthropological Association.

Hefland, David P. 1999. *Career Change: Everything You Need to Know to Meet New Challenges and Take Control of Your Career*, 2nd edition, Lincolnwood, IL, VGM Career Horizons.

Kay, Andrea. 1996. *Interview Strategies That Will Get You the Job You Want*, Cincinnati, OH, Betterway Books.

Kay, Andrea. 1997. *Resumes That Will Get You the Job You Want*, Cincinnati, Betterway Books.

Kimeldorf, Martin. 1997. *Portfolio Power: The New Way to Showcase All Your Job Skills and Experiences*, Princeton, NJ, Peterson's.

Koons, Adam, Beatrice Hackett, and John P. Mason (eds.). 1989. *Stalking Employment in the Nation's Capital: A Guide for Anthropologists*, Washington, DC, Washington Association of Professional Anthropologists.

Krannich, Ronald, and Caryl Krannich. 1998. *Jobs and Careers with Nonprofit Organizations: Profitable Opportunities in the Nonprofit Sector*, Manassas Park, VA, Impact Publishers.

London, Manuel, and Edward M. Mone. 1987. *Career Management and Survival in the Workplace*, San Francisco, Jossey-Bass.

Lowstuter, Clyde C., and David P. Robertson. 1995. *Network Your Way to Your Next Job—Fast*, New York, McGraw-Hill.

Nemnich, Mary B., and Fred E. Jandt. 2001. *Cyberspace Job Search Kit 2001–2002: The Complete Guide to Online Job Seeking and Career Information*, Indianapolis, Jist Works.

Newhouse, Margaret. 1993. *Outside the Ivory Tower: A Guide for Academics Considering Alternative Careers*, Cambridge, MA, Office of Career Services, Harvard University.

Omohundro, John T. 1998. *Careers in Anthropology*, Mountain View, CA,

Mayfield Publishing Co.

Potter, Beverly A. 1984. *The Way of the Ronin: A Guide to Career Strategy*, New York, American Management Associations.

Redfield, Alden (ed.). 1973. *Anthropology Beyond the University*, Southern Anthropological Society Proceedings, No. 7, Athens, University of Georgia Press.

Richardson, Douglas B. 1994. *National Business Employment Weekly: Networking*, New York, Wiley.

Ryan, Alan S. 2001. *A Guide to Careers in Physical Anthropology*, Westport, CT, Bergin & Garvey.

Sabloff, Paula (ed.). 2000. *Careers in Anthropology: Profiles of Practitioner Anthropologists*, NAPA Bulletin No. 20, Washington, DC, American Anthropological Association.

Secrist, Jan, and Jacqueline Fitzpatrick. 2001. *What Else Can You Do with a Ph.D.: A Career Guide for Scholars*, Thousand Oaks, CA, Sage Publications.

Stephens, W. Richard. 2002. *Careers in Anthropology: What an Anthropology Degree Can Do for You*, Boston, MA, Allyn and Bacon.

Stuart, George E. 1986. *Your Career in Archaeology*, Washington, DC, Society for American Archaeology.

van Willigen, John. 1987. *Becoming a Practicing Anthropologist: A Guide to Careers and Training Programs in Applied Anthropology*, NAPA Bulletin No. 3, Washington, DC, American Anthropological Association.

Yate, Martin. 1999. *Knock 'Em Dead 1999*, Holbrook, MA, Adams Media Corp.

## Books on Managing Your Job

Fisher, Roger, and Alan Sharp. 1998. *Getting It Done*, New York, Harper Business.

Fisher, Roger, and William Ury. 1981. *Getting to Yes: Negotiating Agreement Without Giving In*, Boston, Houghton Mifflin.

Harris, Philip R., and Robert T. Moran. 1991. *Managing Cultural Differences,* 3rd edition, Houston, TX, Gulf Publishing Co.

Hyatt, Carole, and Linda Gottlieb. 1993. *When Smart People Fail*, revised edition, New York, Penguin Books.

Mager, Robert F., and Peter Pipe. 1970. *Analyzing Performance Problems*, Belmont, CA, Pitman Learning.

Simons, George F., Carmen Vázquez, and Philip R. Harris. 1993. *Transcultural Leadership: Empowering the Diverse Workforce*, Houston, TX, Gulf Publishing.

Wexley, Kenneth N., and Stanley B. Silverman. 1993. *Working Scared: Achieving Success in Trying Times*, San Francisco, Jossey-Bass.

Willis, Sherry L., and Samuel S. Dubin (eds.). 1990. *Maintaining Professional Competence*, San Francisco, Jossey-Bass.

Winston, Stephanie. 2001. *The Organized Executive*, New York, Warner

Books.
Zey, Michael G. 1984. *The Mentor Connection*, Homewood, IL, Dow Jones–Irwin.

## Books on Ethics

Appell, G. N. 1978. *Ethical Dilemmas in Anthropological Inquiry: A Case Book*, Waltham, MA, Crossroads Press, African Studies Association, Brandeis University.

Beals, Ralph L. 1969. *Politics of Social Research: An Inquiry into the Ethics and Responsibilities of Social Scientists*, Chicago, Aldine.

Cassell, Joan, and Sue-Ellen Jacobs (eds.). 1987. *Handbook on Ethical Issues in Anthropology*, Special Publication No. 23, Washington, DC, American Anthropological Association.

DeMars, Nan. 1997. *You Want Me to Do What? When, Where and How to Draw the Line at Work*, New York, Simon & Schuster.

Fluehr-Lobban, Carolyn (ed.). 1991. *Ethics and the Profession of Anthropology: Dialogue for a New Era*, Philadelphia, University of Pennsylvania Press.

Nash, Laura L. 1993. *Good Intentions Aside: A Manager's Guide to Resolving Ethical Problems*, Boston, Harvard Business School Press.

Punch, Maurice. 1986. *The Politics and Ethics of Fieldwork*, Qualitative Research Methods, Vol. 3, Beverly Hills, CA, Sage Publications.

Rynkiewich, Michael A., and James P. Spradley. 1981. *Ethics and Anthropology: Dilemmas in Fieldwork*, Malabar, FL, Robert E. Kreiger Publishing.

## Books on Writing and Publishing

Appelbaum, Judith. 1998. *How to Get Happily Published,* 5th edition, New York, HarperCollins.

Becker, Howard S. 1986. *Writing for Social Scientists*, Chicago, University of Chicago Press.

Cohn, Elizabeth, and Susan Kleimann. 1989. *Writing to Please Your Boss*, Rockville, MD, PC Press.

Elbow, Peter. 1998. *Writing with Power: Mastering the Writing Process*, New York, Oxford University Press.

Germano, William. 2001. *Getting It Published: A Guide for Scholars and Anyone Else Serious About Serious Books*, Chicago, University of Chicago Press.

Henson, Kenneth T. 1995. *The Art of Writing for Publication*, Boston, Allyn and Bacon.

Howard, V. A., and J. H. Barton. 1986. *Thinking on Paper*, New York, William Morrow.

# WORKS CITED

American Anthropological Association. 1982. *Getting a Job Outside the Academy*, Washington, DC, American Anthropological Association.

Anderson, Geoff, David Boud, and Jane Sampson. 1996. *Learning Contracts: A Practical Guide*, London, Kogan Page Limited.

Angrosino, Michael V. 1981. "Practicum Training in Applied Anthropology," *Human Organization* 40, no. 1: 81–84.

Baba, Marietta L. 1994. "The Fifth Subdiscipline: Anthropological Practice and the Future of Anthropology," *Human Organization* 53, no. 2: 174–186.

———. 1998. "Anthropologists in Corporate America: Knowledge Management and Ethical Angst," *Chronicle of Higher Education*, May 8: B4–5.

Bailey, F. G. 1969. *Stratagems and Spoils: A Social Anthropology of Politics*, Oxford, Basil Blackwell.

———. 1983. *The Tactical Uses of Passion*, Ithaca, Cornell University Press.

———. 1988. *Humbuggery and Manipulation: The Art of Leadership*, Ithaca, Cornell University Press.

———. 1991. *The Prevalence of Deceit*, Ithaca, Cornell University Press.

Basalla, Susan, and Maggie Debelius. 2001. *"So What Are You Going to Do with That?": A Guide to Career-Changing for M.A.'s and Ph.D.'s*, New York, Farrar, Straus, and Giroux.

Becker, Howard S. 1986. *Writing for Social Scientists*, Chicago, University of Chicago Press.

Berreman, Gerald. 1991. "Ethics Versus 'Realism' in Anthropology," in Fluehr-Lobban (ed.), *Ethics and the Profession of Anthropology: Dialogue for a New Era* (Philadelphia: University of Pennsylvania Press): 38–71.

Bishop, Ralph. 1985. "Stones, Bones, and Margaret Mead: The Image of American Anthropology in the General Press 1927–1983," *Anthropology Newsletter* (April): 18–19.

Bodley, John. 1994. *Cultural Anthropology: Tribes, States, and the Global System*, Mountain View, CA, Mayfield Publishing Co.

Bolles, Richard. 1978. *The Three Boxes of Life*, Berkeley, CA, Ten Speed Press.

———. 2001. *What Color Is Your Parachute?* Berkeley, CA, Ten Speed Press.

Brown, John. 1984. "Professional Hegemony and Analytic Possibility: The Interaction of Engineers and Anthropologists in Project Development," in William Millsap (ed.), *Applied Social Science in Environmental Planning* (Boulder, CO: Westview): 37–59.

Bushnell, John. 1976. "The Art of Practicing Anthropology," in Michael V. Angrosino (ed.), *Do Applied Anthropologists Apply Anthropology?* Southern Anthropological Society Proceedings, No. 10 (Athens, GA: Southern Anthropological Society): 10–16.

Chambers, Erve. 1985. *Applied Anthropology: A Practical Guide*, Prospect Heights, IL, Waveland Press.

———. 1987. "Applied Anthropology in the Post-Vietnam Era: Anticipations and Ironies," *Annual Review of Anthropology* 16: 309–337.

———. 1991. "Acceptable Behaviors: The Evolving Ethos of Ethics Talk," in Fluehr-Lobban (ed.), *Ethics and the Profession of Anthropology: Dialogue for a New Era* (Philadelphia: University of Pennsylvania Press): 155–174.

Chambers, Robert. 1993. *Challenging the Professions: Frontiers for Rural Development*, London, Intermediate Technology Publications.

———. 1997. *Whose Reality Counts? Putting the First Last*, London, Intermediate Technology Publications.

*Chronicle of Higher Education*. 2001. October 17.

Cohn, Elizabeth, and Susan Kleimann. 1989. *Writing to Please Your Boss*, Rockville, MD, PC Press.

Corcodilos, Nick. 1999. "Breaking Ranks and Rules: A Headhunter Shows How to Land a Job in Business," *Chronicle of Higher Education*, Spotlight, August 27 (www.chronicle.com/jobs/99/08/99082703c.htm).

Coye, Dale. 1997. "Earnest Boyer and the New American College," *Change* (May-June): 21–29.

Crain, Cathleen, and Nathaniel Tashima. 2000. "You Gotta Have Friends," in Paula L. Sabloff (ed.), *Careers in Anthropology: Profiles of Practitioner Anthropologists* (Washington, DC: American Anthropological Association): 18–22.

David, Kenneth. 1988. "Consulting in Sri Lanka: Developing a Consulting Career," *Practicing Anthropology* 10, no. 1.

Drake, H. Max. 1988. "Being a Bureaucrat: Is It the Same as Being an Anthropologist?" in Karen J. Hanson (ed.), *Mainstreaming Anthropology: Experiences in Government Employment*, NAPA Bulletin No. 5 (Washington, DC: American Anthropological Association): 40–50.

Ervin, Alexander M. 2000. *Applied Anthropology: Tools and Perspectives for Contemporary Practice*, Boston, Allyn and Bacon.

Everett, Melissa. 1995. *Making a Living While Making a Difference: A Guide to Creating Careers with a Conscience*, New York, Bantam Books.

Fetterman, David. 1983. "Guilty Knowledge, Dirty Hands, and Other Ethical Dilemmas: The Hazards of Contract Research," *Human Organization* 42, no. 3: 214–224.

Fisher, Roger, and William Ury. 1981. *Getting to Yes: Negotiating Agreement Without Giving In*, Boston, Houghton Mifflin.

Fiske, Shirley. 1991. "Forward," in NAPA, *NAPA Directory of Practicing Anthropologists* (Washington, DC: American Anthropological Association): v–vii.

Fiske, Shirley, and Erve Chambers. 1996. "The Inventions of Practice," *Human Organization* 55, no. 1 (spring): 1–12.

Fluehr-Lobban, Carolyn (ed.). 1991. *Ethics and the Profession of Anthropology: Dialogue for a New Era*, Philadelphia, University of Pennsylvania Press.

Frankel, Barbara, and M. G. Trend. 1991. "Principles, Pressures, and Paychecks: The Anthropologist as Employee," in Fluehr-Lobban (ed.), *Ethics and the Profession of Anthropology: Dialogue for a New Era* (Philadelphia: University of Pennsylvania Press): 177–197.

Gabarro, John J., and John P. Kotter. 1980. "Managing Your Boss," *Harvard Business Review* (January-February): 92–100.

Gilbert, M. Jean, Nathaniel Tashima, and Claudia C. Fishman. 1991. "Ethics and Practicing Anthropologists; Dialogue with the Larger World: Considerations in the Formulation of Ethical Guidelines for Practicing Anthropologists," in Fluehr-Lobban (ed.), *Ethics and the Profession of Anthropology: Dialogue for a New Era* (Philadelphia: University of Pennsylvania Press): 200–210.

Gordon, Paige. 2000. "An Anthropologist Checks Out the Business World," *Chronicle of Higher Education*, First Person, March 10 (www.chronicle.com/cgi2-bin/printable.cgi).

Greenwood, Davydd J. 2000. "Theory-Practice Relations in Anthropology: A Commentary and Further Provocation," in Carole E. Hill and Marietta L. Baba (eds.), *The Unity of Theory and Practice in Anthropology: Rebuilding a Fractured Synthesis*, NAPA Bulletin No. 18 (Washington, DC: American Anthropological Association): 164–175.

Greenwood, Ernest. 1957. "Attributes of a Profession," *Social Work* 2: 44–55.

Grillo, Ralph. 1996. "Teaching and Learning Social Anthropology," *Anthropology Today* 12, no. 1: 1–2.

Hackenberg, Robert A. 1988. "Scientists or Survivors? The Future of Applied Anthropology Under Maximum Uncertainty," in Trotter (ed.), *Anthropology for Tomorrow*, AAA/NAPA Publication No. 24, Washington, DC, American Anthropological Association: 170–185.

———. 1999. "Advancing Applied Anthropology," *Human Organization* 58, no. 1: 105–107.

Hamilton, James W. 1973. "Problems in Government Anthropology," in Alden Redfield (ed.), *Anthropology Beyond the University*, Southern Anthropological Society Proceedings, No. 7 (Athens: University of Georgia Press): 120–131.

Hess, G. Alfred. 1993. "Testifying on the Hill: Using Ethnographic Data to Shape Public Policy," in David M. Fetterman (ed.), *Speaking the Language of Power: Communication, Collaboration and Advocacy* (Washington, DC: Falmer Press): 38–49.

Holton, Ed. 1998. *The Ultimate New Employee Survival Guide*, Princeton, NJ, Peterson's.

Honadle, George, and Jerry van Sant. 1985. *Implementation for Sustainability*, West Hartford, CT, Kumarian Press.

Hopper, Kim. 1997. "On Contract Knowing: Notes Toward a Taxonomy of Foreclosed Inquiry," *AAA Newsletter* (September): 34–35.

Howard, V. A., and J. H. Barton. 1986. *Thinking on Paper*, New York, William Morrow.

Hyland, Stanley, and Sean Kirkpatrick. 1989. *Guide to Training Programs in Applied Anthropology*, Memphis, TN, Society for Applied Anthropology.

Jenakovich, Marsha, and R. Owen Murdoch. 1997. "A Space of Our Own: The Case for Masters-Level Professional Anthropology," *Practicing Anthropology* 19, no. 2 (spring): 17–21.

Johnsrud, Cris. 2000. "Integrating Anthropologists into Nonacademic Work Settings," in Paula L. Sabloff (ed.), *Careers in Anthropology: Profiles of Practitioner Anthropologists* (Washington, DC: American Anthropological Association): 95–98.

Joseph, Rebecca (ed.). 1997. "A Conversation About Contract Knowing," *Anthropology Newsletter* (September): 10–11, 14.

Kearns, Kevin P. 1992. "From Comparative Advantage to Damage Control: Clarifying Strategic Issues Using SWOT Analysis," *Nonprofit Management and Leadership* 3, no. 1 (fall): 3–22.

Kidder, Rushworth M. 1991. "Academic Writing Is Convoluted, Jargon-Ridden and Isolated from the Messy Realities of the World," *Chronicle of Higher Education*, Section 2 (January 30): B1–2.

Korten, David. 1980. "Community Organization and Rural Development: A Learning Process Approach," *Public Administration Review* 40, no. 5: 480–511.

Loeb, Paul Rogat. 1999. *Soul of a Citizen: Living with Conviction in a Cynical Time*, New York, St. Martin's Press.

Louis, Suzanne, and Joan Atherton. 1982. "The Secret Life of Anthropological Training: A Job Search Strategy," *Practicing Anthropology* 5, no. 1: 20–21.

Mager, Robert F., and Peter Pipe. 1970. *Analyzing Performance Problems*, Belmont, CA, Pitman Learning.

Montell, Gabriela. 2000. "A Look at the Job Market for Anthropologists," *Chronicle of Higher Education* (November 17), online Career Network (www.chronicle.com).

Nash, Laura L. 1993. *Good Intentions Aside: A Manager's Guide to Resolving Ethical Problems*, Boston, Harvard Business School Press.

Newhouse, Margaret. 1993. *Outside the Ivory Tower: A Guide for Academics Considering Alternative Careers*, Cambridge, MA, Office of Career Services, Harvard University.

Nolan, Riall. 1998. "Teaching Anthropology as If It Mattered: A Curriculum for 21st-Century Practitioners," *Practicing Anthropology* 20, no. 4: 39–44.

Omohundro, John T. 1998. *Careers in Anthropology*, Mountain View, CA, Mayfield Publishing Co.

Painter, Michael. 2000. "Nonacademic Experience and Changing Views of the Discipline," in Paula L. Sabloff (ed.), *Careers in Anthropology: Profiles of Practitioner Anthropologists* (Washington, DC: American Anthropological Association): 75–81.

Partridge, William L. 1979. "Anthropology and Development Planning," *Practicing Anthropology* 1, nos. 5–6: 6, 26–27.

———. 1985. "Toward a Theory of Practice," *American Behavioral Scientist* 29, no. 2 (November-December): 139–163.

Peacock, James L. 1999. "Toward a Proactive Anthropology," in Linda G. Basch, Lucie Wood Saunders, Jagna Wojcicka Sharff, and James Peacock (eds.), *Transforming Academia: Challenges and Opportunities for an Engaged Anthropology*, American Ethnological Society Monograph Series No. 8 (Washington, DC: American Anthropological Association): 31.

Peters, Robert L. 1992. *Getting What You Came For*, New York, Farrar, Straus, and Giroux.

Pottier, Johan (ed.). 1993a. *Practising Development: Social Science Perspectives*, London, Routledge.

———. 1993b. "The Role of Ethnography in Project Appraisal," in Pottier, *Practising Development* (London: Routledge): 13–33.

Price, Laurie J. 2001a. "The Mismatch Between Anthropology Graduate Training and the Work Lives of Graduates," *Practicing Anthropology* 23, no. 1: 55–57.

———. 2001b. "How Good Is Graduate Training in Anthropology?" *Anthropology News* (May): 5–6.

Puntenney, Pamela (ed.). 1991. "Commentary: Communicating Anthropological Insights," *Practicing Anthropology* 13, no. 3 (summer): 23–28.

Rynkiewich, Michael A., and James P. Spradley. 1981. *Ethics and Anthropology: Dilemmas in Fieldwork*, Malabar, FL, Robert E. Kreiger Publishing.

Schön, Donald. 1983. *The Reflective Practitioner: How Professionals Think in Action*, New York, Basic Books.

———. 1987. *Educating the Reflective Practitioner: Toward a New Design for Teaching and Learning in the Professions*, San Francisco, Jossey-Bass.

Shankman, Paul, and Tracy Bachrach Ehlers. 2000. "The 'Exotic' and the 'Domestic': Regions and Representation in Cultural Anthropology," *Human Organization* 59, no. 3: 289–299.

Singer, Merrill. 1994. "Community-Centered Praxis: Toward an Alternative Non-Dominative Applied Anthropology," *Human Organization* 53, no. 4: 336–344.

———. 1995. "Commentary: Elitism and Discrimination Within Anthropology," *Practicing Anthropology* 17, nos. 1–2 (winter-spring): 42–56.

———. 2000. "Why I Am Not a Public Anthropologist," *Anthropology News* (September): 6–7.

Stone, John V. 1993. "Professional Networks," *Practicing Anthropology* 15, no. 1 (winter): 25–27.

Sweitzer, H. Frederick, and Mary A. King. 1999. *The Successful Internship*, Pacific Grove, CA, Brooks/Cole Publishing.

Trotter, R. (ed.). 1988. *Anthropology for Tomorrow*, AAA/NAPA Publication No. 24, Washington, DC, American Anthropological Association.

van Willigen, John. 1976. "Applied Anthropology and Community Development Administration: A Critical Assessment," in Michael V. Angrosino (ed.), *Do Applied Anthropologists Apply Anthropology?* Southern Anthropological Society Proceedings, No. 10 (Athens, GA: Southern Anthropological Society): 81–91.

———. 1986. *Applied Anthropology: An Introduction*, South Hadley, MA, Bergin & Garvey.

Winston, Stephanie. 2001. *The Organized Executive*, New York, Warner Books.

Yate, Martin. 1999. *Knock 'Em Dead 1999*, Holbrook, MA, Adams Media Corp.

Zey, Michael G. 1984. *The Mentor Connection*, Homewood, IL, Dow Jones–Irwin.

# INDEX

Academic anthropologist: definition of, 5–6

Academics and practitioners: connections between, lack of, 26, 175; constraints on, 162–163; contrasts between, 16–22, 25–27, 160–161, 174–175, 181; core and periphery, 171; job security, 17; influence on lives of others, 161; job market, academic, 24–25; resentment and suspicion, 159, 160; responsiveness to clients, 21, 160; rewards and constraints, pattern of, 17–18, self-definition, 20–21; work structures, differences, 16–17; tenure, 24; work products, 19–20; work styles, 18–19, 182. *See also* Lone wolf tradition; Status

Accomplishments: interviews, use in, 116, 121–122; professional portfolio, use in, 98–99; resume, use in, 100–102

Advisers, academic: "black halo" effect, 57; choosing, 49, 55–57; and graduate school, 48; reputation of, 57; and younger professionals, 172. *See also* Mentors

Allen, Mitchell, 183

Alta Mira Press, 183

American Anthropological Association, 8, 159; building practice, role in, 172; ethics statements, 157; involvement of practitioners, lack of, 26; and practitioners, 3; presentation opportunities, for practitioners, 183

*American Anthropologist:* lack of, articles on practice, 26

Anthropological advantage: elements of, 10–12; and the job search, 78–79; in marketing yourself, 79, 118–120; and new jobs, 129; in solving human problems, 180

Anthropology Documentation Project, 4, 26–27. *See also* Literature of practice

*Anthropology Newsletter,* 170

Applied anthropologist: definition of, 5–6

Appropriate imprecision: in on-the-job learning, 132

B.A.: practice with a B.A., 36, 38

Baba, Marietta, 30, 159, 163

Base: as a component of practice jobs, 8

Becker, Howard, 154

# ABOUT THE BOOK

How can students and scholars effectively prepare for—and succeed at—a career as a nonacademic practicing anthropologist? This comprehensive guide, full of practical detail, presents the answers.

Nolan relates how students, recent graduates, and beginning professionals can acquire and use the skills essential for work as a practitioner. A key feature of his book is its comprehensive focus: he systematically moves from preparation, to finding one's first job, to career survival and management. The book concludes with a detailed discussion of how to turn a career in practice into a solid contribution to both the profession and the discipline. The result is an important reference for current practitioners—and a must-have handbook for beginning anthropologists.

**Riall W. Nolan** is associate provost and director of the Institute of Global Studies and Affairs at the University of Cincinnati. He has worked as a practitioner for a variety of international development agencies, including the Peace Corps, USAID, and the World Bank. He is the author of *Communicating and Adapting Across Cultures* and *Development Anthropology: Encounters in the Real World.*